To Betsy,

On behalf of the ancestors including Harriet Tubman and abolitionist Sarah Grimké, enjoy.

14 OCT 15

Dining With The Ancestors
When Heroes Come To Dinner

A BLACK HISTORY COFFEE TABLE BOOK

BY

DR. ERIC J. CHAMBERS

WHO DAT?
PUBLISHING
HOUSE, LLC

DININGWITHTHEANCESTORS.COM

Dining With The Ancestors: When Heroes Come To Dinner
©2015 Eric J. Chambers

Published by Who Dat? Publishing House, LLC
A division of Who Dat? Productions, LLC
101 W. Central Avenue * Suite 231
Brea, California 92821

Library of Congress Control Number: 2014922934

ISBN 978-1-4951-3774-7

Edited by Lezlee Hinesmon-Matthews, Ph.D * Loyola Marymount University, Los Angeles, CA

Front Cover Designed by Tanner Gray/Absolut Graphics * Houston, Texas
Back Cover/Interior Designed by Eric J. Chambers * West Covina, CA

Photo credits: Eric J. Chambers, Rochelle Porter, Richard Darryl Nichols, Devonna Law, Harold Corsey, TJ Dunnivant, Nate Payton, Lisa L. Loftin, Keashonna Christopher, Isaac Leggett, Melvin Parker, Shahid Shabazz, Shawna M. Chambers, Aerica N. Chambers, Lisa Lake Grossman, Leonard Delpit, Sherri Bryant, Randall Hooper, Lezl Peters, Tasha Whitten Griggs, Lanee Battle and Erma Byrd.

Frederick Douglass, Harriet Tubman, Major Taylor, Dorothy Dandridge, Emmett Till & Mamie Till photos are public domain.

Additional photo courtesies: Tyler Perry, Nikki Giovanni, T'Keyah Crystal Keymah & Willard Pugh.

Illustration Artists: André Harris, Clarence "Pencilman" Pointer, Michelle Brantley, Mike Fields, Quatrick Williams, Keenan Chapman and Stevon Sample.

Printing Director * Mike McCoy (Jostens, Inc.)
Distributed by BCH Fulfillment & Distribution, 33 Oakland Ave, Harrison, New York 10528

Printed in the United States by Jostens, Inc.

DiningWithTheAncestors.com

THESE ARE MY PEOPLE: 8 Generations Later

This book is dedicated to my ancestors.

The vintage picture of these people on the front cover are my kinfolk. Taken 100 years ago in 1915 in Rose Hill, Mississippi, who knew it would find its way on the front cover of a book eight generations later? Amazing! The day after my grandmother **Lucille Taylor Goodman's** funeral in Rose Hill in June 1987, my great-aunt, **Mary Byrd Bender** explained to me in a videotaped interview who the people were in the picture. She was my great-grandmother **Willie Lee Byrd Taylor's** sister. Their mother, **Calla Johnson Byrd,** is holding an umbrella, standing to the right of the man in the picture, her dad.

From left to right are **Ada Johnson Bender**, my great, great grandmother **Calla's** sister, **Hattie Johnson Lang** (Calla's cousin), **Willis Johnson**, my great, great, great-grandfather, a former slave, holding what appears to be a business book. And to his right is his daughter, **Calla**, my great, great-grandmother. **Louella Lang** is wearing the bow tie. She is Calla's cousin. In the far right, waving her hand, is **Rose Isaac Jordan**, my great, great, great-grandmother, a former slave. Her son, **Mark Jordan,** was my great, great-grandfather and the dad of **Morgan Taylor**, my great-granddaddy. The little girl is a cousin, **Nevada Phillips Dukes**.

Lunch With A Legend:

The picture that inspired this book.

    Mrs. Mamie Till Mobley, the mother of civil rights icon **Emmett Louis Till,** was my guest in San Diego, CA in 2000. Here, I am flanked by **Shawna**, my then-wife, and **Shahid Shabazz**, one of my best friends and Navy buddy. Next to Mrs. Mobley is her late cousin **Abe Thomas,** who accompanied her to San Diego from Chicago.

    Looking at this picture in December 2012 reminded me that I have dined with some of my heroes including Mrs. Mobley, **Sistah Rosa Parks**, **Don Cornelius**, **Frankie Beverly** and **Andraé Crouch**. That thought inspired me to start asking celebrities if they could dine with anyone from our past~or present, who would it be and what would that conversation consist of? I had no idea the question would blossom into this book. Mrs. Mobley would become a "surrogate grandmother" to me. I was honored to speak at her funeral in Chicago in 2003.

Introduction
The Birth of This Book

Emmett Louis Till. His name is synonymous with the heinous killings of young black boys at the hands of racist white men. Called "the sacrificial lamb" of the modern civil rights era, the 14-year-old Chicago boy was brutally murdered on August 28, 1955 in Money, Mississippi for allegedly whistling at a white woman. His death was the tipping point of the civil rights struggle of the mid-1950s.

Though his body was bludgeoned beyond recognition, his mother, **Mamie Carthan Till** opted to have an open casket funeral. "*I wanted the world to see what they did to my baby,*" she said, as her pain was felt around the world. She was her parents' only child and Emmett was her only offspring. Therefore, his killers strangled to death her direct blood line.

Emmett Louis Till and **Mamie Carthan Till**

On the back of this iconic picture Mrs. Mobley sent me personally, she wrote,
"Dec. '54. Our last Xmas!"
Emmett: 7-25-41 - 8-28-55
"From the Mamie Till-Mobley Collection."
(Public Domain/Directly from Mamie Till Mobley)

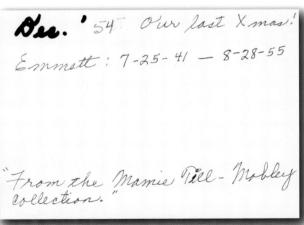

Four months later, on December 1, 1955, **Rosa Parks**, a 42-year-old seamstress, refused to give up her bus seat to a white person in Montgomery, Alabama. As she sat in defiance before her arrest, she thought about young Emmett. This incident galvanized the city's black residents and created an important symbol of the movement: The Montgomery Bus Boycott, which lasted 381 days. It would launch to prominence a young minister named **Rev. Dr. Martin Luther King, Jr**.

This is me and **Sistah Rosa Parks**, another of my heroes, on her 79th birthday, February 4, 1992 at San Diego Mesa College. What a delight it was getting to know her personally!

That's **Sistah Rosa Parks** and **Dr. Jack Kimbrough**, San Diego's first Black dentist, at his home. I shot this picture Monday, February 10, 1992, the same day *Roots* author **Alex Haley** died. Dr. Kimbrough, who was also my friend, called me, saying, "*Eric, bring your camera! Rosa Parks is coming over.*" **W.E.B. DuBois** was his friend too and even stayed at this very home in 1959. He showed me a book W.E.B. autographed! I did a mini TV documentary on Dr. Kimbrough, whose grandmother **Sylvia** was a slave, born at Hermitage in Tennessee and was the black daughter of **President Andrew Jackson**.

I first learned about the Till murder in the summer of 1987 in my US History From A Black Perspective classes at San Diego's Mesa College, where I first met Sistah Rosa Parks, and San Diego City College. My professor, **Alazar Tesfamariam,** showed us the PBS documentary series, *Eyes On The Prize*. Till's story stuck with me like no other. It is a constant reminder of one of the sacrifices that was made for future generations, including mine. Because of my gratefulness to Emmett and the freedom fighters I became determined to vindicate the struggle by doing good in my own life, and not perpetuate the pain by violating the rights of others, including the right to life.

Thirteen years later, in the fall of 2000, while attending Sunday service at West Angeles Church of God in Christ in Los Angeles, our pastor, **Bishop Charles E. Blake, Sr.** introduced special guest **Mrs. Mamie Till Mobley** who was in LA to promote a new play called *The State of Mississippi vs. Emmett Till* which was starting that following Friday at a small 99-seat theatre in LA.

After service I attempted to meet Mrs. Mobley, but she and her cousins **Airickca** and **Ollie Gordon** had already headed to the airport for their return to Chicago. Though disappointed I didn't meet her, just seeing her in person made my day. I'm glad I was at church that day! Otherwise, this book wouldn't have been inspired by what was to come: dinner with a hero.

Photo courtesy of Airickca Gordon Taylor

Bishop Blake and **Mrs. Mobley** flanked by **Airickca** & **Ollie Gordon**.

Airickca is keeping her cousin Mamie's legacy alive as executive director of the Mamie Till Mobley Memorial Foundation. She's a civil rights advocate and have recently collaborated with the parents of Trayvon Martin.

Learn more at
MamieTillMobleyFoundation.org

After dining with **Bishop Charles E. Blake** and **Lady Mae L. Blake**, his bride, we strike a pose. He is the international presiding bishop of the Churches of God in Christ and longtime pastor of West Angeles Cathedral COGIC in Los Angeles. (He also officiated my wedding in 1999.) I'm happy he allowed Mrs. Mobley to greet the congregation. Otherwise, I would have missed my moment to make history.

I took my wife **Shawna Chambers** to the play's opening night in LA. Producer **Spencer Scott** and his cast did a fantastic job portraying the Emmett Till story. After the performance, I asked him what would it take to bring it to San Diego where I host my popular Jazzspel radio show? His answer was simple: "You!" Days later we agreed to a $3000 fee. I was working for the CBS2 News in Hollywood at the time--making good money as a 4-time Emmy/5-time Golden Mike Award winning editor/producer. I wanted to share this experience with my adopted hometown community of San Diego, and with Professor Tesfamariam and my other Black History professors including **Dr. Shirley Weber**, **Professor Starla Lewis, Dr. Nathan Katungi** and **Dr. Dorothy Smith**. Therefore, I made the investment and the rest is history~world history.

About three weeks before the San Diego performance, I called Spencer and asked if he would call Mrs. Mobley in Chicago and ask if she'd come be our special guest. She gave him permission to give me her phone number. I called her and she said she'd be happy to come. I asked how much would it cost me. She said just her airline ticket and one for **Abe Thomas**, her cousin who would assist her. She added if I can make a donation to the Emmett Till Foundation, that would be great. "*That's it!*" I thought. "*We have a deal!*"

A few phone calls later, I asked if I could create an award and name it after her and Emmett. She replied, "*Mr. Chambers, I would be honored if you did that.*" Well, I did. It's called the Emmett Louis Till/Mamie Till Mobley Humanitarian Award and she was the first recipient. **President** and **Mrs. Barack Obama** would be future awardees in 2009. Mrs. Mobley mailed me a letter and the iconic black and white picture of her and Emmett to use to promote the event and award.

Within a few days I bought their plane tickets. Then I called **Reggie Wooldridge**, the hotel general manager at the Ramada Inn in Old Towne San Diego and asked if the hotel would sponsor their room for the weekend. They did. We had the play at San Diego's Educational Cultural Complex October 27 and 28, 2000. It began with a Friday night reception and birthday party honoring Mrs. Mobley, complete with cake, food, music and memories.

Tickets from the San Diego play.

4

Shahid Shabazz, my general manager, drove her from the hotel to the venue. As they arrived, I had all of our guests line both sides of the elevator. When the doors opened, as Abe pushed her in a wheelchair, the people applauded. Mrs. Mobley cried. She was overcome with joy. My heart was touched with compassion to see such love overflowing. The people came to say thanks. It was already a major success if nothing else happened. That night I presented her the humanitarian award named in her honor.

As her cousin Abe pushes her wheelchair to the reception, Mrs. Mobley is surprised to see a crowd of people lining both sides of the aisle applauding her. She wept.

I presented Mrs. Mobley the Inaugural Emmett Louis Till/Mamie Till Mobley Humanitarian Award on Friday, October 27, 2000 at San Diego's Educational Cultural Complex. She's holding the award in her lap as I speak.

Before the play started, we had a wonderful reception in her honor. **Dr. Shirley Weber**, (in white pants), was among my guest speakers. In 2013, she became a California State Assembly member.

Though her birthday is November 23rd, I surprised her on October 27, 2000 with an early birthday cake.

That next day, Shahid, Shawna and I took Mrs. Mobley and Abe to lunch. Before eating, I had a waiter snap a picture of us at the table. Who knew it would inspire this book fifteen years later? Let this serve as a reason why we should sow in each other's dreams. You just never know what the harvest will bring forth.

We had three performances that weekend, including two on Saturday. Mrs. Mobley was present at each show. We didn't have the crowds I hoped for. Therefore, I took a $5000 bloodbath! But it was the best bloodbath I have ever had. And I would do it again! If it was just me, her, the cast, crew and my wife at the play, I would have been at peace. I just wanted to personally honor Mrs. Mobley and Emmett, and this was a wonderful way to do it. Just being in her presence was worth the investment.

On Sunday, October 29, 2000, she worshiped with us at my San Diego home church, St. Stephen's Church of God in Christ. **Bishop George D. McKinney, Jr** was pleased she visited and allowed me to introduce her. She spoke to the congregation, then wept as Bishop prayed for her. Hosting this legend in San Diego and worshipping with her was one of the proudest moments of my life. Seeing her happy gave me great joy. It was a blessing being able to pour into her life after all she'd sacrificed.

To the left, Mrs. Mobley is all-smiles as I introduce her to the St. Stephen's COGIC family in San Diego. In the center, she speaks to the audience and to the right, she's emotional as Bishop McKinney offers a prayer for her.

Hours later as we were about to check her and Abe out of the hotel and take them to the airport, I thanked her profusely. "*Mrs. Mobley, thanks so much for spending this weekend with us,*" I told her. She replied, "*Mr. Chambers, I needed to be here more than you needed me here.*" As we ate the last of her birthday cake before leaving the hotel room, she continued, "*I will never forget the people of San Diego and what they did for me. And Mr. Chambers, you will always have a special place in my heart. That's for sure.*" I shed a tear as I gave her a warm hug, wishing she could stay with us forever. I didn't want the weekend to end.

The only time I was sad was when I gave her an envelope with only $500 in it for the Emmett Till Foundation. I hoped for better attendance at the play so that I could give her more, but she was pleased with what I gave her. The experience was more valuable to both of us than the money. She knew my heart was pure and my intentions were real. From then on, she became a "surrogate grandmother" to me as we often called each other just to say hello. For some reason, she always called me "Mr. Chambers." I have a video of her giving my wife motherly advice on the phone, offering her experience as Emmett's mother.

Spencer Scott, producer of the play *The State of Mississippi vs. Emmett Till* share a moment with Mrs. Mobley.

SD Mesa College's Black Studies Professor **Starla Lewis** says hello.

Dr. Dorothy Smith was honored to meet her.

Dr. Shirley Weber offers expressions.

The **Penny** Family drove nearly 200 miles from Oxnard to San Diego to support Mrs. Mobley and I.

SD 4th District Council member **Rev. George Stevens** declared it Mamie Till Mobley Day in SD and presented her a sign that read "Welcome to San Diego."

During her San Diego visit, I made sure I captured the essence of the weekend by interviewing **Mrs. Mamie Till Mobley** on video for my future TV show, on audio for my current radio show and still pictures in case I wrote a book some day. Well, 15 years later, "some day" has come.

THE TEAM: **Abe Thomas**, **Shahid Shabazz** and **Lanee Battle** made sure Mrs. Mobley was taken care of that weekend.

The cast from the play, *The State of Mississippi vs. Emmett Till.*

San Diego pastor **Dr. Steve O. Cooper** was among those who supported this effort.

I hope my daughter Aerica will one day cherish this picture and share it with future generations: Her daddy and mommy Shawna, a Delta Sigma Theta, hosting Mrs. Mobley in SD.

Mrs. Mobley was elated to receive the first Emmett Louis Till/Mamie Till Mobley Humanitarian Award in San Diego.

Mrs. Mobley autographs a copy of the book, *A Death In The Delta* for Shawna and I, although she told me there were some inaccuracies in it. Notice she still signed on behalf of Emmett and her cousin Abriel.

A Death in the Delta

To Eric & Shawna:
Thank you for a blessed trip and for all the love you have shown!
Mamie Till-Mobley
10-28-00.
Emmett & Abriel

9

The Death Of A Legend

On January 6, 2003, my friend **Karen Hill** called from Chicago to tell me Mrs. Mobley died that afternoon. I was devastated. I was scheduled to call her that night to confirm another visit with me. When I learned the funeral date, I began shopping for airline tickets. The prices ranged from $800 - $1500. It appeared I wasn't going to be able to attend. Then, the day before her wake I was about to head to San Diego from LA when I was led to bid on Priceline one more time. It accepted my bid, a round trip, non-stop ticket from LAX to Chicago, leaving the next day, for only $287! It was a sign I was meant go bid farewell to this woman I grew to love.

On my way to the airport I called Karen to tell her I was coming to Chi-town after all. She wasn't home but her grandfather, **Elder George Liggins** answered. *"Oh! I know you. You're the one with the radio show in San Diego huh? My granddaughter told me about you."* He was Mrs. Mobley's pastor at Evangelistic Crusaders Church of God in Christ in Chicago and they were planning the funeral. Little did I know, that quick, 90-second call from an airport shuttle would grant me an experience of a lifetime.

I stayed at my cousin **Barbara Adams'** home in nearby Country Club Hills, Illinois. As her then-husband **Spencer** drove me to the funeral at Apostolic Church of God, I wondered how people lived in such a cold place! It was 5 degrees with a windchill of -13 below zero! When we arrived at the church, I was shocked to see they had a coat-check service. I'd only seen something like that at a swanky club or restaurants in Beverly Hills. Though my overcoat was thin by Chicago standards, I checked it in.

I started shooting video in the lobby. Then I saw my friend **Elaine Eason Steele**, the lady who cared for Sistah Rosa Parks until her death. After a few minutes videotaping, I went upstairs to the balcony with the rest of the media. To my surprise, during the middle of the service, **Rev. Jesse Jackson**, who was officiating the funeral, asked, *"Is Eric Chambers here?"* Again, I was in the balcony facing right in front of him. Then he said, *"Show me some sign. Show me some sign."* Once he saw me waving, he asked me to come on down to speak. I was in awe! I was just happy to be there. But to speak? Wow!

I spoke after former presidential candidate **Carol Mosely Braun's** remarks, and was introduced by former presidential candidate Rev. Jackson. Talk about shocked! I shared the story about Mrs. Mobley giving my wife motherly advice before our then-seven month old daughter **Aerica** was born. As I spoke, I cried. I cried because I loved Mrs. Mamie Till Mobley like she was my own grandmother. I cried because I was going to miss our long phone conversations and hearing her call me "Mr. Chambers." I cried because she wasn't going to come visit us in Southern California again. I cried because my soul ached and my heart was broken cried because I still couldn't believe that I, a poor, welfare kid from New Orleans, by way of Pearl River, LA, who was raised in a trailer that got repossessed, was speaking at the funeral of a civil rights legend I learned about in the history books!

Rev. Jackson closed out the service asking for the Gatling undertakers to *"come and do your work now,"* as the Evangelistic Crusaders Choir sang. *"She's going to be with Emmett now!"* Rev. Jackson shouted in a rhythmic, Baptist hoop. Off in the distance you can hear someone say, *"Yeah!"* He continued, *"She's going to be with the Father now."*

I gathered my camera gear and ran back downstairs after the recessional. Though it was freezing, I didn't get my overcoat because I needed to videotape the casket being put in the hearse and didn't want to miss it. People were dressed in fine, expensive furs while I had on my cheap blue double-breasted LA Garment District suit. As I got my last shots of the flowers being put in the hearse, a lady wearing a matching mink hat and coat looked at me without my overcoat and shook her head saying, *"He can't be from around here!"* She was right. I came from Hollywood, but I needed those shots for history's sake.

Then, moments later, another lady tapped me on the shoulder and said, *"I'm **Rita Fannings**, the administrator at Evangelistic Crusaders Church and Elder Liggins is my dad. He told me to make sure you spoke."* That answered my own question of how I got on program. As Spencer and I drove to Burr Oak Cemetery for Mrs. Mobley's burial next to **Genie Mobley**, her late husband, and about 40 yards from Emmett's final resting place, I was amazed at how a short, 90-second phone call thrust me into a footnote of Mrs. Mobley's history! I thank God for Elder Liggins allowing me that golden opportunity. (Ironically, on February 19, 2003, just over a month after Mrs. Mobley's funeral, he died on his 86th birthday.)

After we arrived in the long car line at the cemetery, I jumped out of the vehicle, this time wearing my thin overcoat and ran to shoot video of the black, horse-drawn carriage carrying Mrs. Mobley by her son Emmett's grave one last time. After a two-man Army color guard placed flowers at the site, and a short Rev. Jackson prayer, we proceeded to her tomb. I almost didn't feel my hands anymore! They say the stinging sensation was the early stage of frostbite. Even with gloves on, my hands were numb~and stung! But as a single drummer drummed an ancestral African song graveside, we all braved the bitter cold to sing one last song, pray and say goodbye to Mrs. Mobley.

In June of that year, 2003, I debuted my Jazzspel TV show on The Word Network. I served for 9 years and did 137 episodes. Even with all of my credentials as a 4-Emmy/5-time Golden Mike Award winner from CBS, The Word Network never paid me. But I always remembered what Bishop McKinney told me: *"The Lord is going to honor your faithfulness."* Although my wildly popular show cost them nothing, and it was star studded from Hollywood, the network canceled it in March 2012.

In November 2012, I struck a verbal deal to go to another TV station, TCT (Total Christian Television). They called me December 11, 2012, the day after my birthday, and said they're picking up my show for their network. I was at Sam's Club in La Habra, CA when I got the call and had to sit down to rejoice.

I called my mother, **Hester Jordan Ducre** in Pearl River, LA and my brother **Lorenzo Chambers** in Albuquerque to tell them the great news. I was going to a new network! In anticipation of my February debut, I started pre-planning for a Black History month special. One day while looking at a bunch of pictures from Mrs. Mobley's visit to San Diego in 2000, one caught my attention. It was a snap shot of me at lunch with her in Downtown San Diego with Shawna, Shahid and Abe. As my heart missed her, I was grateful I had a chance to have dinner and lunch with one of my heroes. She was my modern-day **Harriet Ross Tubman**, as she led my people in her own special way.

About three weeks later, TCT reneged, sending me a "Dear John" e-mail. Then, I began putting more focus on my own online TV Network, The CUT (Chambers Urban TV Network). In fact, I started getting better gigs because my show was no longer a "religious" show. As I continued to report from red carpets, I asked, **'If you had a chance to spend an evening at dinner with anyone from our black history past, who would it be and what would you discuss?'** *"What a great question!"* quipped pop star and actress **Brandy**. *"What a great concept for a book!"* she offered as we chatted in Beverly Hills in April 2013. Her enthusiastic reaction and those from phone conversations and e-mails with my dear friends and actresses **Dawnn Lewis, Pauletta Washington, Bern Nadette Stanis, Ja'Net DuBois,** and **T'Keyah Crystal Keymah**, and my buddy **Willard Pugh,** who played "Harpo" in *The Color Purple,* is what made me feel that this could be special. As I told **Charlie Wilson**, **India Arie** and **Cedric The Entertainer**, *'You all are heroes to many. This book will let your fans know who their hero's heroes are.'*

Well, here it is~with pictures, quotes, illustrations and Black History facts. I hope it inspires you as much as it inspires me. I honor God for **Mrs. Mobley** and her son **Emmett**, as well as **Sojourner Truth, Justice Thurgood Marshall, Congressman John Conyers, Dr. Ralph David Abernathy, Rev. Jackson, Sistah Rosa Parks** and all of the people who sacrificed so much for the good of Black folk and most importantly, mankind. And let me not forget the White abolitionists and countless others who risked it all in an effort to end slavery or Jim Crow law such as **Chaney**, **Goodman** and **Schwerner, Fannie Lou Hamer** and **Viola Liuzzo**. And I offer special thanks to the likes of **Muhammad Ali, Jackie Robinson** and modern-day abolitionists like **Congresswoman Maxine Waters, Congressman John Lewis,** the late **Congresswomen Shirley Chisholm** and **Barbara Jordan,** and former **Ambassador Andrew Young, General Colin Powell** and **The Obamas**. Who knew the DNA for this book would be traced back to an obscure Black History class that I took in 1987? Said **John L. Mason**, one of my favorite authors and publishing mentors, *"This isn't just Black History, but American History. You have yourself a winner."* All I can say is, *'Wow!'*

My message? Invest in the visions of others and it will return greater than your best expectations. I sowed into Spencer Scott's and Mrs. Mobley's visions. All these years later, it's harvest time and it promises to be plentiful. Because of that decision, I will be forever linked to my personal hero: Mrs. Mamie Till Mobley. Ya see Mrs. Mobley. I didn't forget you. Yours and Emmett's legacies lives on.

Finally, if I could dine with anyone from the past and/or present, I'd have an Oprah-style legends lunch and invite **Jesus**, **King Solomon**, **Harriet Tubman**, **Dr. King**, **Frederick Douglass**, and **Nat Turner**. I'd invite Mrs. Mobley again, this time with Emmett along with white abolitionists **Sarah Grimke**, **John Brown** and **William Lloyd Garrison** just to thank them. **Oprah** and **The Obamas** would sit at this very long dining table along with **Frankie Beverly**, **Gladys Knight**, **Patti LaBelle**, **Whitney Houston** and my late friend **Andraé Crouch**, who I'd request sing, "My Tribute." I have to add **Michael Jackson's** party of eight that includes **Sarah Vaughn**, **Sam Cooke**, **Bobby Womack**, **Mandela**, **Marvin Gaye**, **Teddy Pendergrass** and **Minnie Riperton.** I'd ask her to sing "Perfect Angel" and "Can You Feel What I'm Saying." **Bishops McKinney**, **Blake**, **TD Jakes**, **Pastors Cecil "Chip" Murray**, **Rick Warren**, **Billy Graham** and my late grandfather, **Rev. Archie Jordan** would be there to assist Jesus in blessing the food. The table's gonna be tight, but it's gonna be right! Plus, I'd have my late grandmother **Lucille Taylor Goodman** join us, and my mother **Hester Ducre**, and **Ronald Chambers**, my mom's first child who died from crib death at five months young before the rest of us other four children were born. It would be nice getting to know him and thank him for watching over us from the heavens.

I'd have my beloved daughter **Aerica Noelle Chambers** present. I'd want her to meet my heroes, hear their stories and record them for history's sake, then share the updates on Instagram, Twitter, Snapchat, Facebook, You Tube, etc. Ohhh, what a time we'd have breaking bread together! And I know Gladys and Patti would cook up something juicy for us to eat, including some waffles and wings! I'm trying to get a few more seats added to perhaps invite you. So, be patient with me. After it's over, before Jesus gives the benediction and look around at the beautiful array of people, I'd ask a favor of Frankie Beverly: sing "We Are One," for regardless of color, creed or religion~in God's eyes, we are one.

Now, enjoy the answers from some of your favorite actors, singers, athletes, ministers and other notables as told to yours truly. By the way, who would you invite to dinner and what would your conversations consist of? Visit our website at DiningWithTheAncestors.com and write us. You never know. You could win a chance for dinner with a hero or celebrity!

ERIC J. & AERICA NOELLE
CHAMBERS

Tyler Perry,
Movie Mogul/Actor/Playwright

"There were three civil rights workers who were murdered in Mississippi (**Andrew Goodman, James Earl Chaney** and **Michael Schwerner**). Two of them were Jewish (and one, a Black man.) I'd like to ask them about their fears and the courage that it took to go to Mississippi in the face of Jim Crow. And I'd like to thank them for it."

FBI/PUBLIC DOMAIN

ANDREW GOODMAN, JAMES CHANEY & MICHAEL SCHWERNER

Taraji P. Henson,
Academy Award Nominated Actress

TARAJI'S FIRST NAME MEANS "HOPE" IN SWAHILI, AND PENDA, HER MIDDLE NAME, MEANS "LOVE" IN THAT SAME LANGUAGE.

"I would have to say the **Freedom Fighters** because if it were not for the people who risked their lives for our freedom as African-Americans, where would we be? I'd have to ask them, 'How did they have the faith that they had?' Like Dr. Martin Luther King, Jr., it's the faith of God's love when a man spits in your face, and being able to channel God's love, and not retaliate in anger. I don't know if I'm that strong. So, that's the first question I would ask."

WITHOUT A SHADOW OF A DOUBT, TARAJI IS ONE OF HOLLYWOOD'S BRIGHTEST STARS. EXPECT MORE BIG THINGS FROM HER.

"Dr. King is my cousin."

Gladys Knight,
Legendary Singer

"If I could have dinner with anyone from the past, it'll be three people: My **mom**, she's not with me anymore and I miss her tremendously, because she shaped this and formed this and taught me everything. **Dr. (Martin Luther) King** is my cousin and I wish he was still here. And I would like to have dinner with him again. And **Maya Angelou**. We spent a lot of time together and she was one of those people who reached out and wanted the best for everybody, but especially for our people."

Dr. King, Kendrick Lamar & Malcolm X dining on a private jet while discussing blatant racism.

Keenan Chapman,
Illustrator

Kendrick Lamar,
Rap Music Sensation

"I know a lot of people say **Martin Luther King**, but I would say **Malcolm X**. I would ask him when do I really know when to hold 'em and when to fold 'em,'" he says with a smile. "How to control the temper and turn it into something positive because sometimes things get to us, especially as an artist. Especially as a Black man. I can get on a plane tonight and sit in first class and a woman will even clutch her purse and ask how did I get there. It's been asked before. I've been asked that numerous times. It's a lot to control that and still stay respectful and stay with some dignity. I do it. But sometimes out of frustration I might slip and say something else. I would ask Malcolm how to control that. I would ask Martin Luther King how to control the temperament when you're asked silly questions that still involve racism. I feel it's still alive~just a little bit. It's still there in a sarcasm way. I think what they~MLK & Malcolm instilled in me is so much pride and dignity, it's hard to try to run away from that, so I may get a little frustrated sometimes."

Kendrick & I share a laugh in LA.

Roslyn M. Brock,
Chairman of NAACP

Admiral Michelle J. Howard,
Vice Chief of Naval Operations

At the 2014 NAACP Image Awards in LA, I interviewed the NAACP's **Roslyn M. Brock** and **Admiral Michelle J. Howard**. On July 1, 2014, she became the first woman to achieve full admiral in the US Navy. On that same day, she became the 38th Vice Chief of Naval Operations. I told her we both joined the Navy the same year, 1982, and she thanked me for my service. Then I joked, *"But you did a whole lot better than I did!"* She smiled. She received the NAACP's Chairman's Award at this event. I'm SUPER proud of her~and Roslyn. Shine brightly for the ancestors ladies!

"I would choose to dine with **Ida B. Wells Barnett** and probably discuss her comment about being "the agitator that keep the waters troubled." After all, she was considered to be 'a lion in the den.'"

~Roslyn M. Brock

Former NAACP President **Ben Jealous** & **Roslyn**.

Brandy, Singer/Actress

ERIC J. & BRANDY IN BEVERLY HILLS, CA.

WHITNEY HOUSTON

"I would love to have dinner with **Whitney Houston** just one more time. She is forever in my heart and soul. Forever my fairy Godmother. I love her."

Singer/Actress **Brandy** was one of the first celebrities to enthusiastically encourage me regarding this book. She's a true sweetheart of a star.

Footnote In History

In 1619, the first 20 Africans, indentured servants, arrived in North America in Jamestown, VA. It was a year before the Mayflower landed at Plymouth Rock, MA.

Dawnn Lewis and **Cleopatra** dining.

André Harris,
Illustrator

"I would love to meet **Cleopatra** because of her intellect, power and beauty in a time when she ruled a nation. What an amazing woman she was! She inspired cultures around the world that people wanted to emulate her. She was a force of nature. She set a bar that would change the world. She brought nations to their knees. She was so awesome, historians wished she was white and have tried to undo her Africanness. I'd ask her, 'How did you do it?' I want to be as smart and resourceful as you. She was in love with **Marc Antony**. It's so relevant to today's woman who is in power. It's hard, challenging to be a woman in a male-dominated society. But her success as a female is inspiring."

Dawnn Lewis,
Actress/Singer

Dining with **Dawnn,** my dear, respected friend, better known as "Jaleesa" from *A Different World.*

Rev. Jesse L. Jackson, Sr.

Civil Rights icon & 2-time Presidential Candidate

Rev. Jackson and I at the Beverly Wilshire Hotel after his birthday gala, November 20, 2014.

"I would want to have dinner with **Dr. King** again. I'd ask him what's next, because he could always see around the curve."

~Rev. Jackson

Rev. Jackson meets the press with **Nina Rawls**, widow of singer **Lou Rawls**, after Lou's funeral at West Angeles COGIC in January 2006. Nina is my friend and supporter.

I first saw Rev. Jackson at Southern University in Baton Rouge, LA when I was a freshman there in 1980. Since then, I have worked with him and interviewed him many times. He's one of my favorite icons in the world. I am forever grateful for all the good he has done.

Rev. Jackson and I talk NAFTA at the Tubman/Chavez Center in San Diego in 1994 when I was news director at Smooth Jazz 98.1 KIFM radio.

Nelson & Winnie Mandela (Public Domain)

Bishop TD Jakes,
Pastor/Author/Movie Mogul

"I WOULD LIKE TO HEAR THE INSIDE STORY. WHAT IT COST YOU TO BE YOU."

"**Nelson Mandela**. **Dr. Martin Luther King**. **Harriet Tubman**. **Harry Belafonte**~who's living. There are a lot of people that I would like to sit down and talk to because they survived at a time~most of them~when life was tough. And I would like to hear the inside story. The stories that are not written. What it cost you to be you. We chronicle what you accomplished, but never how much you paid to do it. How much of your life did you give up to make the world a better place? And how do you reconcile in your own human need, as a finite being, the use of your days to move the world and then lay down your life. And, is it enough to be appreciated in an encyclopedia? And **Nelson Mandela**, How did you balance the natural propensity for revenge after the apartheid and the swelling anger that existed in South Africa against the far loftier and more important ideal of sustaining the country? And what did it take to hold those two truths to end perfect tension? Those would be some of the conversations."

Chatting with **Bishop TD Jakes** in LA's Westwood.

22

In an interview on the **Jimmy Kimmel** show, actor **Morgan Freeman** talked about one of his heroes, **Bass Reeves**, who's believed to have been the nation's first black federal US Marshal. Under difficult circumstances, Reeves arrested over 3000 people including some of that era's most dangerous criminals. He even arrested his own son for murder!

Morgan Freeman,
Actor

US Marshal Bass Reeves

Morgan Freeman, one of my favorite actors, and I in Beverly Hills after interviewing him for the movie, *"Olympus Has Fallen."*

Born in 1838, Reeves, a former slave, fought with his master then fled to Indian Territory to avoid punishment. He lived among the Seminole and Creek Indians until the Emancipation Proclamation freed slaves in the confederate states in 1863. Upon retirement in 1907, Reeves had spent 32 years as a federal officer. He died January 12, 1910.

23

Giving Honor To The Legends

Louis Gossett, Jr.
Academy Award Winning Actor

HARRY BELAFONTE, LOUIS GOSSETT, JR. & SIR SIDNEY POITIER AT THE NAACP IMAGE AWARDS IN LOS ANGELES, FEB. 17, 2012.

*"I've met many people since I was seventeen, from **Lena Horne** to **Josephine Baker** to **Paul Robeson**. I've been with **Dr. Mandela**. So I suppose my choice should be **Mahatma Gandhi** and my great grandmother. She lived to 112 years old. I've been very fortunate. Another I would like to have met is **Ira Aldridge**, the first Black Shakespearean actor ever. He was great. Look him up!"*
~Lou Gossett, Jr.

Legendary actor **Louis Gossett, Jr** won an Emmy for his role as "Fiddler" in the TV mini-series *Roots*. He's with his friend **Shirley Neal** at an Oscar viewing party at the Beverly Hills Hotel.

SNAPSHOT FOR HISTORY: BROTHERLY HUG

THE MEN WHO PAVED THE WAY.

IN 1964, SIR SIDNEY POITIER BECAME THE FIRST BLACK PERSON TO WIN AN OSCAR FOR BEST ACTOR. LOUIS GOSSETT, JR WON AN ACADEMY AWARD FOR BEST SUPPORTING ACTOR IN 1982. SINGER/ACTOR HARRY BELAFONTE WAS A CONFIDANT OF DR. MARTIN LUTHER KING.

Yolanda King,

Actress/Daughter of Martin Luther King, Jr. and Coretta Scott King

"Well, I have to give all praise and due respect to my mother, **Coretta Scott King**. In fact, my father always said, 'If it had not been for her courage and her bravery; her wisdom and tenaciousness, he wouldn't have been who he was.' She's tough as nails, but soft. My mother grew up with a father whose life was threatened on a regular basis, so she already had the muscle. She was ready when she married **Martin Luther King, Jr.** It was not a coincidence. When things got tough, she wasn't afraid like some women would have been, or people would have been. She was like, 'Oh, I'm used to this. We're fine. I am fine. I'm not going anywhere. I'm here with you.' And, thank God for her! A magazine, US World News & Report, did a survey and next to **Jesus**, the most popular man in the world was Martin Luther King, Jr."

I interviewed my late friend **Yolanda King** in LA on May 19, 2004. She was the first person I asked the question that's the subject of this book. That was 10 years before I knew it would be a book! She died unexpectedly in 2007.

EVEN HEROES HAVE HEROES

FREDERICK DOUGLASS CALLED DR. SMITH

"The single most important influence on his life."

DR. SMITH

MR. DOUGLASS

Footnote In History

In 1837, **Dr. James McCune Smith** became America's first black physician. He graduated at the top of his class at Scotland's University of Glasgow and became the first black person to run a pharmacy in the United States. An apothecary, author and abolitionist, he helped Frederick Douglass start the National Council of Colored People in 1853.

Howard Hewett,

Singer

ME, **HOWARD HEWETT** AND **DEXTER KING** (SON OF DR. MLK) IN BEVERLY HILLS.

"I would like to sit down with **Dr. King**, mainly to see if we implemented his dream the way that he thought about it. Once he started talking about the economy, economic freedom and economic equality, that's when he was kinda ex'd off. I would like to sit down with him to see where his head was at as far as how we were to implement what he was really starting to go into. He might not have been thinking anywhere past the mountaintop. I don't know. I personally don't think that he meant for us to try and assimilate ourselves into the white race or equality or whatever. But it meant more to be right along side them because we are an economic force that we haven't even realized that we are. That would be an interesting conversation."

~Howard Hewett

Charlie Wilson,
Legendary Singer

"It'll probably be **Nelson Mandela.** I'd ask why did his country hate him so much? They just locked him up in this small box 27 years. What is it they didn't want you to say? And why they didn't want you to say it? I would love to just hug him though. For real. And I would love to shake hands with **Dr. Martin Luther King**. I remember **Coretta Scott King** wanted our song, "Someday" to be the theme song when they were trying to get the Dr. Martin Luther King holiday. **Stevie Wonder's** sang it with me and played the harmonica. It was incredible. We were just with some people at that time that just didn't see the vision. I just look back at it now and it's like, man, we were in bed with the devil."

India Arie,
Singer

"It would be all of the people I consider world transformers: **Martin Luther King**, **Ghandi**, **Nelson Mandela** and **Jesus,** because I believe Jesus was black. And both of my grandmas. They're not Black History but they are to me. The conversation would be all about all the things I need to know to fulfill my mission in this lifetime. Something I'm serious about, the mission that I carry with my life through my music at this time, I would love to hear how to do it better."

Sheryl Underwood,
Comedian/TV Host

Michael Fields, Illustrator

Sheryl Underwood and **Marlon Wayans** stands by for the "Judgement Day" verdict as Eric J interviews to **The Lord.**

Sheryl Underwood's guest would be **Jesus**. And what would she ask? "Am I gonna get in?" she said with hilarity. "You said Black History past, Jesus is always in our past. So, I'm gonna sit down and talk to the Lord. But really, I would thank him for interceding so we can have eternal life. I'd definitely do that. Then I'd ask the Lord, 'How's it lookin' for me?'" she said boisterously.

Continuing seriously, "I hope that one day "The Talk," (her daytime CBS TV show) will become a vehicle where we can have more discussions about faith. One thing I love about being on CBS and being on The Talk, it's one of my most favorite subjects to speak about. You know it's okay for me to be funny, but to talk about the Lord and to talk about how much I love the Lord and how much I'm trying, and not get eyes rolled at you. My colleagues are **Julie Chen**, **Sarah Gilbert**, **Aisha Tyle**r and **Ms. Osbourne**, you know with what she's going through, for her to allow us to say that we're going to lift her up in prayer. When you're looking at what's happening to **Valerie Harper**. She is ready to take the next journey. So, to have a vehicle like "The Talk" and where you can speak about what the next journey is going to be, it's fantastic! Praise the Lord!" Back to joking she added, "And anytime y'all need me to come do something in a church, I will come~and clean up the language! I do stuff for religious people. I love the Lord. And if I can become a first lady, that would be fantastic!"

29

Essence Atkins & Marlon Wayans
Actress   Actor

Essence: **Malcolm X**.

Marlon: **Martin Luther King**. I would love have a conversation with Martin about his journey and patience and him pursuing that dream. But before those two, honestly, **Jesus**. I would like to sit down and talk to JC.

Essence: Yeah, it would be really cool to talk to Jesus.

*Essence & Marlon were the first two celebs I asked this direct question for the book.

Nadege August
Actress

"I would love to share a simple meal of collard greens with international superstar **Eartha Kitt**! She made her way to Europe through **Katherine Dunham** (my #2) and had the foresight to recognize and share the magnitude of her talents by walking away from Ms. Dunham's troupe in order to become what America would not let her be in the 1950's. In 1968, her career in America suffered after she made anti-war statements at a White House luncheon hosted by **Lady Bird Johnson**. I would ask her about her bold move during the White House luncheon and her "come back." I regret never being in the presence of her light in her latter years as she went on to perform yearly at The Carlisle Hotel in NYC."

Footnote In History

Benjamin Banneker, the son of a free woman and a former slave, built the first American-made clock in 1754, although he had never seen one. He built it by carving each piece to scale, based on a borrowed pocket watch. It kept perfect time for 20 years. A farmer, surveyor, mathematician, astronomer, almanac author and scientist, Banneker had little formal education and was self-taught.

Cedric The Entertainer,
Comedian/Actor

CEDRIC AND I AT STEVE HARVEY'S HOLLYWOOD WALK OF FAME STAR UNVEILING.

"There's some great people in our history that I'd like to sit with. I would want **Malcolm** and **Martin** there at dinner. I'd love to sit with **Frederick Douglass**; And **Marcus Garvey** is somebody that I feel I'd want to do a movie with. I'd ask what was the mindset of him thinking you can be in the shipping business--to be a forward thinker at a time when oppression was the norm, when to not think past your own neighborhood as the idea. You thought about world travel, globalization and economics. For Martin and Malcolm, the spirit of seeing the culture in the country when there was so much oppression, so much uncivilly in the civil rights world; just to hear their true thoughts on how do we get the job done? I think there's some validity to both of their approaches. There are a lot things that go with nonviolence and there is a lot of power to building yourself up from inside your community and trusting that. You see it in other cultures, be it Jewish or Asian, and they keep it all inside and build up their cultures. Is it something to the assimilation of wanting to be like the other cultures? Do you feel like you lose yourself? I'd like to ask those questions."

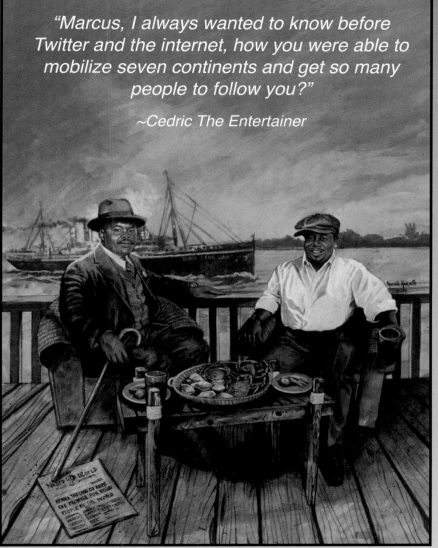

"*Marcus, I always wanted to know before Twitter and the internet, how you were able to mobilize seven continents and get so many people to follow you?*"

~Cedric The Entertainer

Marcus Garvey & **Cedric** with the Black Star Line ship in the background.

Ne-Yo,
Singer

I interviewed singer **Ne-Yo** at an Oscars party in Beverly Hills in 2014 for my online TV network, The CUT: Chambers Urban TV Network.

"**Dr. King** is who I would choose. I just want to know what he'd think about our progress from then until now."

Footnote In History

In 1623, **William Tucker** was born. He is believed to have been the first black child born in North America.

Good Times dining with **Bern Nadette Stanis**, aka "Thelma."

Bern Nadette Stanis,
Actress

Bern Nadette's late mother **Eula** was her rock.

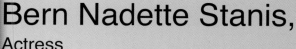
Paul Robeson

"I would choose opera singer **Paul Robeson** because I think he was an awesome, super human man. He had a great, deep voice. He was a great singer. I'd like to know how did he feel being all alone in the world at that time? He was way ahead of his time. A serious actor and activist, he was so fabulous. I'd also love to sit with my mom **Eula**~and her mom, my grandmother **Louise**. I would want to find out who she was. When she passed I was seven. My mother was a writer and I'm a writer and I wanted to write for my grandmother. She never got a chance to really do it. She was so young when she had my mother. I write for them now."

Quatrick Williams, Illustrator

"...aint I a woman..."

Sheryl Lee Ralph, **Yolanda Adams** and **Tamar Braxton** all chose **Sojourner Truth**, the abolitionist and women's suffrage movement leader.

"Wow! I'd have to have a round table. I'd have **Sojourner Truth**, **Madam CJ Walker** and **Mary McLeod Bethune**~women who made a difference. And I would glean all of the knowledge that they have, to find out how I can make a difference now and beyond."
~**Yolanda Adams**

34

Yolanda Adams,
Gospel singer

Yolanda Adams, my longtime friend.

Tamar was pregnant during this 2013 interview in Downtown LA.

Tamar Braxton-Herbert,
Singer/TV Personality

The colorful **Tamar** is always fun to talk to.

THE REAL, Real!
This is us at the 1995 Soul Train Music Awards after-party in Santa Monica, CA. We've both persisted in this business, though it hasn't been a "gravy train with biscuit wheels."

"The person that's popping out right now is **Sojourner Truth**. I would just like to know her journey, how she got over so many things. And her strategy! She was probably one of the smartest people in the world."

35

MC Lyte,
Rap Legend

"I would pick **Lena Horne**. I would want to know what it was like to be her at a time when things were so much more different for our people. I'd want to know how she made it through the struggle."

LENA HORNE, FROM HER OWN STAGE SHOW, NINE O'CLOCK REVUE IN 1961.

MC Lyte, one of my favorite rappers and I at a party in Beverly Hills, September 2014.

Public Domain/Library of Congress

Fast & Furious! **Tyrese** visits with me for a moment at a post-Academy Awards party in Beverly Hills in 2014.

Dr. King and Malcolm X, March 26, 1964

Tyrese Gibson,
Singer/Actor

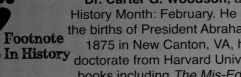

Footnote In History

Dr. Carter G. Woodson, a writer, journalist and historian, is the Father of Black History Month: February. He pioneered Negro History Week in 1926 to coincide with the births of President Abraham Lincoln and Frederick Douglass. Born December 19, 1875 in New Canton, VA, he became the second African-American to receive a doctorate from Harvard University, behind only **Dr. W.E.B. DuBois**. He wrote many books including *The Mis-Education of the Negro*. He worked diligently to preserve Black History and had an extensive collection of publications and artifacts.

DR. CARTER G. WOODSON

37

Willard Pugh,
Actor

"My dinner guest would be **Marshall "Major" Taylor**. He became the first black world champion cyclist in 1899. He had such a high "code of living." It was so inspiring, it made me want to change the standards of my own life. After going through what he went through, including racism, it never altered his behavior. I'm not sure I could have done it. That brother stood strong! He was a great man. **Joe Louis** would be another I'd want to sit with. He gave a million dollars to the war cause, but at the end of his days, he was in trouble with the IRS over taxes. Other than my father, those two guys have had the biggest impacts on my life."

Public Domain

WILLARD PUGH IS A NATIVE OF MEMPHIS AND CAME INTO PROMINENCE AS "HARPO" IN THE MOVIE, "THE COLOR PURPLE," PLAYING SOPHIA'S (OPRAH WINFREY) HUSBAND.

WILLARD SHARES A LAUGH WITH STEVIE WONDER AT THE BILL PICKETT RODEO IN LA.

Nicknamed "The Black Cyclone," Major Taylor dominated cycling in the early 1900s, drawing thousands of fans to stadiums worldwide, including Madison Square Garden in New York. He won his first race at age 13.
LEARN MORE AT MAJORTAYLORASSOCIATION.ORG

"I'd love to have dinner with **The Obamas**. They're not past. They're current. But I think they're extraordinary. The president and the first lady. I love her too. She's an extraordinary woman. I would just love to hear them talk about anything. They're both very eloquent and intelligent. I would just like to hear their views on so many things. Their daughters are amazing too."

Lisa Leslie, Former Pro Basketball Player

Antonique Smith, Singer/Actress

"From our Black History past, I would say **Jesus**. I have no idea what color Jesus was, but I believe in Him and that's who I would love to spend time with. I would also say **Dr. Martin Luther King** and **Gandhi**. I just think they were two men with great minds of peace and they just thought of different ways to really evoke change."

39

Guy Torry,
Comedian

"I would love to have a conversation with my dad. I just lost him on Friday (Jul 11, 2014). There's so many things I wish I could have asked him. So, that's my hero. That's my number one celebrity. I'd ask him how can I be a better man? If I could be half the man that he was, how can I do that? He's the greatest man other than **Jesus** to walk this planet earth. I'll do anything to have one more dinner with my pop."
~Guy Torry

*(Too emotional, and choked up in tears, he abruptly ended his time on the red carpet. His dad's funeral would be days later.)

Dennis Haysbert,
Actor

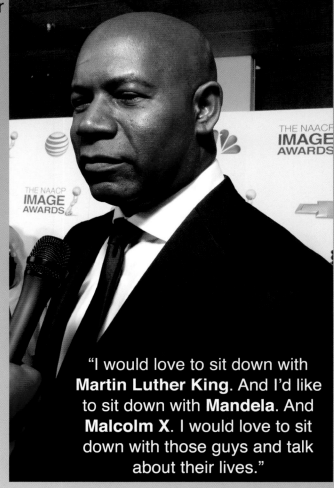

"I would love to sit down with **Martin Luther King**. And I'd like to sit down with **Mandela**. And **Malcolm X**. I would love to sit down with those guys and talk about their lives."

Public Domain
Marion S. Trikosko/
Library of Congress

Footnote In History

In 1721, a smallpox epidemic broke out in Boston. **Onesimus**, an African slave, taught **Cotton Mather**, his Puritan master, an inoculation practiced in Africa. It helped save lives and combat the disease that was sweeping the city.

Jill Scott
Singer/Actress

Jill Scott and I strike a pose backstage at the Shrine Auditorium in Los Angeles at the NAACP Image Awards.

"My choice would be **Nelson Mandela**. Why? Because I have a lot of questions. Because I'm angry."

 Footnote In History In 1645, the Boston-based slave ship "Rainbow" became the first ship to trade directly with Africans, cutting out the West Indies middlemen.

41

"I would start with **Jackie "Moms" Mabley** because I recently saw her documentary and I would ask her why and how in a man's world in comedy~and a foul mouth, did you do it? And how were you that strong? And then I would probably go to **Harriet Tubman** and ask, 'Weren't you afraid? What was in you that made you go back for more? Did anyone ever come back for you?' And the third person I would go back in history to talk to would probably be **Aaron Douglas**, a very famous African-American artist. He was an impressionist and did the mural at my university. You can't really live that way being an artist. What inspired him to make his paintings in just blue and just shapes?"
~Kym Whitley

Robi Reed,
TV/Film Executive

Kym Whitley,
Comedian

"My heroes growing up were my mother and my father. But if I could go back to a time in the past it would be the Harlem Renaissance and I would love to be hanging with **Zora Neale Hurston**, **Langston Hughes**~sipping coffee and philosophizing."
~Robi Reed

Chante Moore,
Singer

My first sit-down celebrity interview was with Chante in 1992 in Hollywood. It aired on KGTV (ABC) in San Diego.

Public Domain

DOROTHY DANDRIDGE

"The first person I thought about was **Dorothy Dandridge**. She broke so many barriers being a Black woman at that time. **Lena Horne**, I'd like to talk to her. And I'd like to talk to **Oprah**. She has changed the face of TV period! I met her one time but I intend to meet her again. We're gonna sit down and have coffee or something! I would just love to learn from all of the women of strength. I'm grateful I am opening doors for other people like they've opened for me."

43

Public
Domain

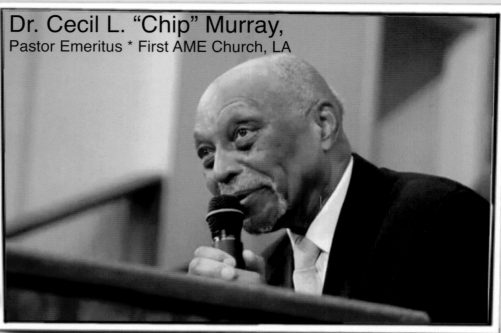

Dr. Cecil L. "Chip" Murray,
Pastor Emeritus * First AME Church, LA

Bishop Richard Allen founded the A.M.E. Church in Philadelphia, PA in 1794.

The African Methodist Episcopal Church was America's first independent black religious denomination.

44

"I'd have dinner with **Richard Allen,** the founder of the AME church. He was a slave who led the first walk-out. The other person would be my dad, **Edward Wilder Murray, Sr**. He was the principal of our school in the deep, segregated south of West Palm Beach and Lakeland, Florida. He was determined that all the students of his schools would get the best of instructions in spite of the fact that the books were hand-me-downs. The students were seated two to a seat. The library was small and inadequate. But he and the faculty would demand the best of every single one of us. We had a graduation rate that exceeded 90% and of those graduating, a good 80% finished college. I have a brother and sister and we all went to school under his leadership, then on to college. He died at age 52. My mother was not in education, but she was the secretary and executive director of the first housing project, Dunbar Village in West Palm Beach, Florida. She (**Minnie Lee Murray**) was our stepmother because my mother, **Janie Belle Murray**, died when I was a year and half old. I remember her as being an extraordinarily, caring person. I spent ten years in the Air Force on duty in a two-seater jet fighter interceptor. After 10 years, my wife and I agreed that it was time for me to go into ministry because that had been the calling of my life. So, we separated from the Air Force and I went to seminary, earning my doctorate at the School of Theology in Claremont, CA. And Eric J., you are a hero. And we are here to feast with you at the dinner."

Malinda Williams,
Actress

Actress **Malinda Williams** of "Soul Food" and "High School High" fame ponders who from history she would invite to dinner.

"I want **Muhammad Ali**, **Martin Luther King**, **Billie Holiday** and **Frederick Douglass**. I want Frederick first! I want **Harriet Tubman**. I want **Nat Turner**. I mean, really! I got questions! And they've got stories! I like stories!" she said with a smile.

The Williams Sisters: **Malinda Williams**, **Lisa Williams Sorenson** and I at H.O.M.E. in Beverly Hills, CA at an event to raise awareness about kidney disease.

Footnote In History

During World War II, **Dr. Charles R. Drew**, a black surgeon, pioneered blood transfusions and organized the first large-scale blood bank in the U.S. He fought against racial segregation in blood donations and out of protest, quit his role with the American Red Cross. The Charles R. Drew University in LA is named in his honor.

45

Dave Winfield,
Pro Baseball Hall of Famer

Jackie Robinson at 1963 March on Washington which featured Dr. King's I Have A Dream speech.

I'm speaking with **Dave Winfield**, a pro baseball Hall-of-Famer and **Tonya**, his wife, in Hollywood at the movie premiere of *42: The Jackie Robinson Story*.

"I'd have **Martin Luther King** on one side along with **Jackie Robinson** and **Malcolm X**. There's a lot of heroes, but Jackie Robinson would be one of them. Absolutely. You're asking me a question that I asked his wife, and his son and his daughter today. I'd ask Jackie to give me one tidbit--something that I can take with me to tell other people. I'd like to know what he was like and what he was all about. In a whole evening, I'd sure enough find out about that. But I know what his legacy means. So, I'm good with that."

~**Dave Winfield**

Clarence "Pencil Man" Pointer,
Illustrator

Roland Martin, **Malinda Williams** and **John Amos** breaking bread with **Frederick Douglass** in his log cabin.

A GOOD TIME CHATTING WITH "JAMES EVANS."

John Amos,
Actor

"That's an interesting question. More than likely it would be with **Frederick Douglass**. Because of what he came from and what he became in terms of our history. I would want to sit and talk to Mr. Douglass until he told me, 'Man! Shut up and go home!'"

> *"If there is no struggle, there is no progress."*
>
> ~Frederick Douglass

FREDERICK DOUGLASS, CIRCA 1879

Kareem Abdul Jabbar,
Pro Basketball Hall-of-Famer

"Jeez, that's a tough one, but I'd probably choose **Frederick Douglass**.
I'd like to know what gave him the courage to be the man that he became."

Footnote In History

In 1834, **Henry Blair**, a slave in Maryland, patented a corn planting machine. But years later, in 1858, the federal government ruled no slave can hold a patent.

Roland Martin,
TV Journalist

"It probably would be **Frederick Douglass**. I would ask him what was it like to be so adamant that you taught yourself to read even knowing full well you could face death if they found out."

~Roland Martin

Dr. Bobby Jones
Gospel music impresario

"I would dine with **Dr. Thomas A. Dorsey**. He was the founder of gospel music. How could I not relate the importance of what it would mean for me to sit and and speak with him? And the **Rev. James Cleveland**, of course. I'm going to stay in the spiritual realm most of the time. And I'd choose **Dr. Maya Angelou** and **Minister Louis Farrakhan**. Those are two of my dearest friends. Diversity there!"

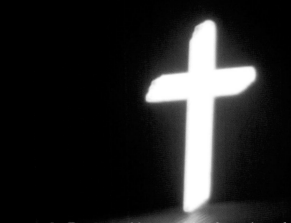

49

Ja'Net DuBois,
Actress/Singer/Painter

Michelle Brantley,
Illustrator

Actress **Ja'Net DuBois** dines with **W.E.B. DuBois**, sociologist, historian, civil rights activist, publisher and co-founder of the NAACP in 1909.

I'm interviewing actress **Ja'Net DuBois**, my "Hollywood mom," at Next Dimension University's graduation on August 17, 2013 in Ontario, CA where we both received doctorate degrees together.
I did red carpet interviews in my robe!

"I would want to have dinner with my grandmother **Elizabeth Gouedy**. I'd like to know if she is proud of me. She used to tell me stories of hers and my mother's life and about slavery. I wonder if she'd be proud of my achievements. She told me, 'You're gonna be my star.' And I'd like to sit with **W. E. B. DuBois**. I want to know if we are related. He used to say, 'Don't hang out with people you don't want to eat with. Don't move too fast.'"

50

Kurt Carr,
Gospel Singer

Kurt Carr at the BET Celebration of Gospel in Downtown LA.

"**Harriet Tubman**. I was just telling my group I'm obsessed with her and the fact that she was free and kept going back~even after she got her family. That's the sign of a true leader and the heart of a Christian person. That is the epitome of what a Christian is about~helping other people. And the fact that they walked from the South to Canada sometimes! That's a long way to walk. And to keep going back. I can talk all day about it. I actually met some of her family in upstate New York. Her house is there. I never got to go to where she's buried, but I went to the house and met some of her family. That's the one!"

Nephew Tommy,
Steve Harvey Show Comedian

"Maybe **Harriet Tubman**, just to figure out how you had a mindset to do what you did and keep going back and forth and getting as many people as you can?"

Public Domain

HARRIET TUBMAN

"I would choose **Jack Johnson**. He was a remarkable man. He was a smart man who was way ahead of his time. I'd love to sit with him and talk, not just about him being the first black man to win the heavyweight boxing championship, but about his business interests."

Julius "Dr. J" Erving,
Pro Basketball Hall-of-Famer

Kellita Smith,
Actress

"It would probably be **Malcolm X** ~and **Jesus**. I would be Jesus' girlfriend. Oh my God! I'd be making him sun block for his long trips. I would cornrow his hair. You know that's why he was dark. Have you ever walked the desert? Are you kidding me? **Mary** would be in trouble, honey! I'd be like, 'We're either gonna share Him honey or He's mine!' Any man who can make a two-piece fish dinner and feed 5000 people, and heal the blind~and make some wine out of water! That's~my man!"

I love this sistah! She keeps me laughing! Talk about hilarious!

Footnote In History

In 1862, **Mary Jane Patterson** became the first Black woman to receive a B.A. degree when she graduated from Oberlin College in Oberlin, Ohio.

I'm flanked by my friends, actresses **Kellita Smith** and **Bonita Brisker**, who does a phenomenal one-woman **Billie Holiday** show. We're at **Vesta Williams's** funeral at West Angeles Church of God in Christ in LA.

53

Photo by ©S. Bukley/ DepositPhotos

Marion "Suge" Knight,

"I would want to have dinner with my grandfathers. First, my mom's dad, **Charles**. My grandfather wrote the song "Corina, Corina." That's one of the reasons I wanted to start a publishing company because so many people, including my granddad, got beat out of their publishing. I'd also like to have dinner with my paternal grandfather, **Thomas Knight,** who had 12 kids, only 3 girls. He made sure he taught his sons to be men, work hard and take care of your family. He was smart enough to teach them love. If you pushed up against him, you had six to eight Knight guys looking for you. So, my foundation started off with two strong men in Vicksburg, Mississippi. I'd also like to sit with **Sam Cooke** and **Bobby Womack**. And with **Malcolm X**. I like the fact that he wasn't afraid of the truth. He wasn't afraid to change. When he went to Mecca, he discovered he had brothers and sistahs with blonde hair and blue eyes. I'd ask him what's the difference between loyalty and being an idiot. And when do you know? How do you know when it's time not to be loyal to something that's not loyal to you?"

INTERESTING TIDBITS:
In our conversation at dinner at the Beverly Hills Hotel, Suge told me he loves gospel music, especially traditional. But I found it quite interesting that this rap mogul is not a fan of gospel rap. Also, did you know he was a standout defensive end for the University of Nevada @ Las Vegas (85-86) and in 1987 played in the NFL for the Los Angeles Rams?

Donnie McClurkin,
Gospel singer

Pastor Donnie McClurkin shares his thoughts with me at the Orpheum Theatre in Downtown LA.

"It would be **Frederick Douglass** because I read his unofficial autobiography as well as all of the biographical things that they wrote. I found him to be most interesting with his attempts to always be free. How he learned how to read and nobody knew it; How he took the knowledge that he had once he came up north and he became so key in politics in changing the whole of society. That's who I'd like to sit and talk to."

COMING TO AMERICA

Footnote In History

In 1839, **Joseph Cinqué**, whose African name was **Sengbe Pieh**, lead 53 slaves in a mutiny aboard the Spanish slave ship *Amistad*. Born in 1814 in what is now Sierra Leone, Cinqué demanded the navigator return the ship to Africa. Instead, it came to America where he and the Africans were charged with mutiny and murder. With former president **John Quincy Adams** as their attorney, the Supreme Court of the US ruled in their favor saying they mutinied to regain their freedom after being kidnapped and sold illegally.

55

Nikki Giovanni,
Poet/Professor

HER FAMOUS SAYING:

"I'm sick and tired of being sick and tired."

Public Domain Library of Congress

Fannie Lou Hamer

Photo courtesy of Nikki Giovanni

"I would want to have dinner with **Fannie Lou Hamer**. She was the founder of the Mississippi Democratic Freedom Party. We would talk about voting. The fact that we have 18-year-old voters is attributed to her. **President Lyndon B. Johnson** offered her two seats at the Democratic Convention and she refused to comprise. My sister and I met her and delivered lunches to the workers. She loved eating and it would be a pleasure to have dinner with her."

Dr. Bernard Kinsey,
Black History Aficionado/Philanthropist

Dr. Bernard & **Shirley Kinsey** of LA have one of the most extensive collections of Black art and Black History artifacts in the world, including a copy of the Dred Scott Decision. Their collections are on tour throughout the nation including at Walt Disney World in Orlando, Florida. To learn more about them, visit TheKinseyCollection.com

*"I would choose to have dinner with some people most have never heard of including **Belinda Royall.** She was born in Ghana, West Africa in 1712 and was kidnapped from her home when she was 12 and made a slave."*
~Dr. Bernard Kinsey

Belinda **R**oyall recalled the horror of slave trade in her 1783 petition, writing, *"An armed band of white men took many of my countrymen in chains."* An Englishman named **Isaac Royall** bought her and she served as a slave in his home in Massachusetts. When he abandoned his slaves, returning to Nova Scotia, Belinda, at 63, challenged the status quo, petitioning the legislature for compensation for her years of service to her former master. The General Court awarded her an annual pension of fifteen pounds and twelve shillings. When their master abandoned them, all of his slaves were declared free. Belinda Royall became one of the first slaves to ask for reparations, suggesting she had a right to pay for her work.

R&B singer **Kem** has such an inspirational story.

Kem,
Singer

Kem and I speak at **Halle Berry's** gala in Beverly Hills.

"**Martin Luther King**. And I'd love to have dinner and a conversation with **Sammie Davis, Jr.**"

In 1760, **Jupiter Hammon** became the first African-American writer published in the United States with the release of his poem, *An Evening Thought: Salvation by Christ with Penitential Cries*. Born October 17, 1711, his masters educated him, although it was illegal. His last known home, 73 West Shore Rd in Huntington, NY is currently under consideration for a historic designation. Hammon was a devout Christian. In one of his poems he wrote, *"If we should ever get to Heaven, we shall find nobody to reproach us for being black, or for being slaves."*

Footnote In History

Public Domain

JUPITER HAMMON

"I had dinner with **George Benson** and **Al Jarreau**; I'll probably want to have dinner with **Stevie Wonder**. And then I want to move to the piano, pull out a guitar and play one of his tunes. In this world, besides **Jesus Christ**, my Lord and Saviour, there's only one guy that I can say is my hero~and it's Stevie. He's timeless. It's like, there's Berklee College of Music and Stevie. He is my Berklee, but also a mentor in many ways. I'd want to ask him, 'What do you feel when you sing? The same with **Tina Turner**. What do you feel when you let it go. What is it? The pain? The suffering? The struggle?' Because those are all the things that you hear and the things that move me. But nothing tops meeting **Nelson Mandela**. I met my president and I was in tears. It was the most amazing thing. And I sang for him. So, Stevie and Nelson Mandela."

Jonathan Butler,
South African Singer/Guitarist

"THERE'S BERKLEE COLLEGE OF MUSIC AND STEVIE WONDER. HE IS MY BERKLEE. BUT ALSO A MENTOR IN MANY WAYS."
~Jonathan Butler

I'M INTERVIEWING **STEVIE WONDER** AND HIS DAUGHTER **AISHA MORRIS** AT THE BET CELEBRATION OF GOSPEL IN LOS ANGELES.

Footnote In History

George Washington Carver was an agriculture chemist and inventor. Born a slave, he discovered over 300 uses for peanuts. Tuskegee Institute's **Booker T. Washington** convinced him to come serve as the school's Director of Agriculture.

G. W. CARVER

"Original Dream Girl" **Loretta Devine** and I share a laugh on the red carpet at an Oscars viewing party in Beverly Hills, CA.

Loretta Devine,
Actress/Singer

"I would say the late **Congresswoman Barbara Jordan** because she was from Houston and I grew up in Houston, Texas and her name is a name I heard all the time and I aspired toward being like."

Ernest Harden, Jr. & Kimberly Elise on the red carpet.

"After doing a play, I really have an affinity for Billie Holiday. She had such a life, but yet she overcame so much. Even though she went down with drugs, she overcame childhood abuse from her family, and everything, and she'd be so interesting, and yet, her talent was~she was a consummate singer. Some of her music is pertinent to music today. She did things back then that we don't even do today. She really made her stamp on music. It would just be great to have dinner and talk to her."
~Ernest Harden, Jr.

Ernest Harden, Jr,
Actor

Footnote In History

In 1773, **Caesar Hendricks**, a slave, sued **Richard Greenleaf**, his Newburyport, Massachusetts master, for "detaining him in slavery." He won the case before an all-white jury! He was awarded his freedom, monetary damages and court costs.

Laz Alonso, Actor

Actor **Laz Alonso** with former "Deception" co-star **Meagan Good** at the NAACP Image Awards in LA.

*"That's such a wide open door. I feel that **Malcolm X** and **Martin Luther King** were taken way too early. I would have loved to have picked their brains and learn what they were really thinking about the situation. Not what they said in their speeches, but what they were really internally feeling at those moments in time. But I don't have to go that far back. Even if I can sit down now and kick it with **Muhammad Ali**! He is an icon. And when you see our icons fall like **Michael Jackson** and other iconic images that will never be replaced, it really makes you value the ones we still have living. It makes you appreciate them. Don't wait until they die to appreciate them. Let's appreciate them now. I think Muhammad Ali is one of those."*

Meagan and I backstage at the NAACP Image Awards.

61

Marla Gibbs,
Actress/Singer

"The person I'd choose to dine with is **Beah Richards**, a great actress whom I loved dearly. She played my mother~twice. I really loved her."

~Marla Gibbs

"One of the incredible, legendary comedians: **Marla Gibbs**. I love Ms. Marla. She is the reason why I speak seven languages now. She was our first **Lucille Ball**. So, I know if I had to be funny, I had to be multilingual funny. People don't know Marla is also a trained dancer and a singer. But she just focused and honed in. Then her blessings came through *The Jeffersons* and her acting. But this woman is so phenomenal. Not only is she a phenomenal talent and actress in general, but she's a phenomenal human being. And to be able to honor her while she is still living and to be blessed by her presence. And I see her often and she's always saying encouraging words to me, and being such a wonderful spirit. She's a genuine good person and I just love her. The work that I've done is a reflection of her amazingness and her grace. And I just praise God for her."

~Beth Payne

Beth Payne,
Comedian

Maryum "May May" Ali,
Producer/Muhammad Ali's daughter

"**Malcolm X**! I wanna talk to that brotha. With the passage of time, I'd ask him what would be a preliminary plan to galvanize black folk to help each other and be self-sufficient. I'd like to come up with a comprehensive strategy for that!"

Daughters of
"The Greatest!"

"It would probably be my own father, **Muhammad Ali**, because he doesn't speak so well anymore. I can't communicate with him the way I would like to. So it would be nice to be able to sit down with him and have a conversation about his past and his experiences and how he views the world now~to take some of that in. That's something that I won't have. Of course, I can read books and listen to old tapes and everything. But it would be nothing like having that one-on-one conversation with my father when he was younger in his prime."

Laila Ali,
Former boxer/Muhammad Ali's daughter

63

"Oh my gosh! **Jesse Owens** for sure. I have his autograph and I'm not going to tell people where it is because it's one of my most treasured things. I would love to just talk to him and just see how it was running in the Olympics in Berlin, because I ran in that stadium before. I would just love to dine with him."

Public Domain

Jesse Owens at 1936 Berlin Olympics.

Lori "LoLo" Jones,
Olympic Track Star

Stevon Sample,
Illustrator

Kelly Price & gospel great **Mahalia Jackson**.

Kelly Price & Lil' Mo
R&B Divas

Kelly Price and **Lil' Mo** at the BET Celebration of Gospel in LA.

"**Mahalia Jackson**, because for me she represented a God movement that touched every area of life, every genre of music. She touched into films. She was church. She represents church today. She's one of the staples and foundations of modern-day gospel and Christian music. And she went into a lot of places that typically traditional Gospel signers could not go. But she took the gospel of Jesus Christ in song with her there, even when the church said she didn't belong in those places. But she carried God with her and I appreciate her for that. I feel like she is the reason a lot of doors have been opened for all of us."

~Kelly Price

~Lil Mo

"I would say **Madam CJ Walker** just because she invented the pressing comb. I bet she can get those edges laid for the king!" **Lil' Mo** said with laughter. Chimed in **Kelly Price**, "Shout-out to Madam CJ Walker! Cleaning kitchens~globally!"

65

Omarosa,

Reality TV Personality

*"I would want to break bread with **Jesus**!"* Omarosa said emphatically with a huge smile. *"I would want to sit down with my Lord and savior!"*

Omarosa is all-smiles when talking about The Lord!

Omarosa snaps a pic of her mom and **Gladys Knight** backstage at the Shrine Auditorium in Los Angeles at the NAACP Image Awards.

Candice Glover,

American Idol Winner

"I would choose **Dr. Martin Luther King, Jr., Rosa Parks** and the singers as well, **Marian Anderson**, **Mahalia Jackson**, all of them. I would like to just see what that period was like and what they had to go through. They paved the way for everything that we're doing now. I definitely look up to them."

Dr. T'Keyah Crystal Keymah,
Actress/Singer

Director/Producer **Chip Hurd**, (one of my favorite people in Hollywood), with **Ervin Hurd**, her husband, **Dr. T'Keyah** and I after watching *"The Passion Play,"* an incredible Easter performance directed yearly by Chip at Shepherd of The Hills Church in Porter Ranch, CA.

*"Wow! With far too many superior choices to ever decide, one greedy scenario would be as follows: Appetizers with **Don Cornelius** to start, while we continued to work on the sitcom idea he had for me. Soup and salad would be next, with my dear friend **Rosalind Cash** along with **Ruby Dee**. The highest compliments I have ever received were comparisons of my work to theirs. I would ask them for more advice on navigating the entertainment industry while balancing personal integrity, civic responsibility and professional success. The main courses would be shared with **Harriet Tubman**, **Toussaint L' Overture** and **Queen Hatshepsut**. Ms. Tubman could tell me what she thought of our 'post racial' police state and how I might better accept the things that I cannot change. The gentleman could offer a glimpse on how I might have the courage (and unparalleled strategies) to change the things I can. I would seek the queen's council on knowing the difference, and also on fair governance and peaceful reign...just in case I am ever needed to rule, In Black World. Duets with **Marvin Gaye**, **Gregory Hines** and **Michael Jackson** would be the perfect dessert. I would discuss with Mr. Gaye and Mr. Hines how to properly bare one's soul on stage with no net, and with Mr. Jackson how to find the discipline to construct of oneself a perfect performer. An after dinner cordial would be shared with **Mahatma Ghandi**, to converse about the transition into true freedom with a peaceful heart. I wish he were at my dinner table every time I watch the news."*

"Maybe **Harriet Tubman**. I learned a lot about Harriet. My daughter's doing a wonderful project on her. She rocked, man! She was the first woman to lead male soldiers in war time. Harriet rocked!"

Lorraine Toussaint,
Actress

"If I could have dinner with anybody in history? **Jesus**! He and I would sit down and break some bread. We'd have a nice dinner and I'd ask Him to do the prayer."

Hill Harper,
Actor/Activist

Mary Wilson,
Singer

"I'm doing a tribute to **Lena Horne** right now and it's touring around America and she would be one of the women I'd dine with. There would be quite a few. My mom is at the top of that list, but celebrity-wise, Lena Horne. I spent time with her. I knew her~not very well, but I knew her. And she was one of the most giving, beautiful women in showbiz and there were lots of them. There were the **Dorothy Dandridges** and **Ethel Waterses**. There were all kinds of them, but I would choose Lena. I wouldn't have to ask her anything because I have pretty much lived the same kind of life, but she did come from a time when as a human being, as a woman, as a celebrity, she didn't receive the kind of accolades that she should have because Blacks were not equal. I would be interested in asking her exactly how that made her feel. Did it take anything from her as a human being, which I know it did, because she had gone to the top, but still she wasn't treated equally as other people were. The one thing about it is we all come on someone's shoulders. And to know we as Black people have had so many great human beings who have succeeded in life and for us to have that history to learn from is a great thing. So we know that we didn't do this all by ourselves."

Mary Wilson, formerly of *The Supremes,* discusses the life of **Lena Horne**.

Footnote In History The first black community was established by indentured servant **Anthony Johnson** on 250 acres in Northampton County, VA in 1651.

Matt Barnes,
Pro Basketball Player

&

Gloria Govan,
Reality TV Personality

NBA player **Matt Barnes** and **Gloria Govan**, his wife, at the *42 Jackie Robinson* movie premiere in Hollywood.

*"I'm going to catch you a little off-guard. Mine is **Tupac**. Not only for the music but because he was really a leader. He was very intelligent and well-informed on the political issues. Well-informed in music. I really just feel that he had the whole package. I would have just encouraged him to tone it down a little bit so that he could be here today."*   **~Matt Barnes**

*"I would have a tie between **Malcolm X** and **Martin Luther King**. My dad is a history major, so, I'm really interested in history. I've always been brought up with history. But I think I would just want to really to spend a day with them. I don't know what I would necessarily want to ask them. I think just to shadow some of the times in their peak of whatever it is that they wanted to do. I think in general they were both amazing men like **Jackie Robinson** who really paved the way and really helped America and the world in general open their eyes to people of color and diversity."*

Gloria Govan~

Sheree Fletcher,
Reality TV Personality

*"Oooh, that's a good question! We've got so many greats in our history, but **Dr. Martin Luther King** comes to mind. I would ask him did he know when he gave his "I Have A Dream" speech. Did you know that it would become larger than life?"*

Nicole Murphy,
Reality TV Personality

"Oh my God! Oooh! I would say **Martin Luther King**. And I don't know what the conversation would be, but it would be quite interesting," she says with laughter and a wide smile.

Footnote In History

Paul Cuffee, a 21-year-old free black man refused to pay taxes in Massachusetts because free blacks didn't have the right to vote. He petitioned the government in 1780 to end taxation without representation. It was denied but lead the way to voting rights in 1783.

Bishop George D. McKinney, Jr.
COGIC General Board Member

Bishop McKinney at **Sistah Rosa Parks'** book signing in San Diego in 1992.
COGIC/Public Domain

Bishop McKinney & Lady Barbara J. McKinney

"I would like to talk to **Bishop C. H. Mason** about his vision for the Church of God in Christ and the kingdom of God. And about how God shaped his spirituality. I'd ask **Mary McCleod Bethune** how she, as a woman, when women were not considered equal with men, was able to get the courage to follow the dream that God put into her mind. As for **Mandela**, I'm still fascinated by the fact that after 27 years of imprisonment and the loss of family, he was able to keep a Jesus attitude regarding forgiveness. And how his practice of forgiveness and love made the difference between a nation being destroyed by racial and class struggle to a nation making a transition guided by love and tolerance."

Bishop CH Mason

Bishop Charles Harrison Mason
September 8, 1866 - November 17, 1961
Founded the Churches of God in Christ, now with over 7 million members.

Bishop Gilbert E. Patterson, the late COGIC presiding bishop and I doing a radio interview in San Diego.

72

*Bishop McKinney, my longtime pastor, ordained me an elder in the COGIC on October 23, 2011.

Sheryl Lee Ralph,
Actress

"**Sojourner Truth** and the first Black women that participated in the women's suffrage movement. If I can sit down with those women because I know what they had to go through. People often think, well they came from Howard University and they went downtown. Do you know what it took for them to leave the campus of Howard University and go down to the capital? What they braved? I was like, 'Who were those young women?' Sojourner Truth! To follow all those White women around, to bear her breast and say '*Ain't I a woman*?' I want to know who were those women. What was really going on?"

Isabella "**Bell**" **Baumfree**,
aka **Sojourner Truth**.

Vincent Hughes
Pennsylvania State Senator

"**Nelson Mandela**. I got arrested in 1985 demonstrating at the South African Embassy in Washington, DC on behalf of breaking down apartheid. We visited South Africa and saw the work he was doing there and leading that country in terms of transition. It would have to be Nelson Mandela. Absolutely."

Senator Vincent Hughes and his wife, Sheryl Lee Ralph met on a blind date set up by friends.

73

David Mann
Comedian/Actor

"The one person I'd invite is **Muhammad Ali.** If I saw him, I'd scream like like a little girl!"
~David Mann

Tamala Mann
Singer/Actress

Take Me To The King!
Tamala's song became a Gospel music hit!

The two have been married over 25 years and still love each other greatly. "*He keeps me laughing,*" she told me.

"Probably **Ms. Rosa Parks**, to just talk about the struggles. I know our struggles don't add up nearly to what they went through, but the foundation that they laid for us, to just be a woman to stand behind her words and not take no for an answer. The bottom line is that's what it was all about. She just didn't take no for an answer. If I could just thank her. That's why I'd want to sit down and have dinner with her."

74  **Footnote In History**   In 1812, the Methodist church sent out an order to all slave owners who want to be ministers: Free your slaves. (My family's church, Mt. Jordan United Methodist Church in Rose Hill, Mississippi is more than 160 years old and was started by **Fred Jordan**, a former plantation owner.)

Farrah "Cocoa" Brown,
Comedian

What a delight it was having lunch at Oprah's OWN Studios and interviewing cast members from Tyler Perry's *For Better Or Worse*.

"I would love to talk to **Coretta Scott King, Martin Luther King** and **Malcolm X**. I'd want to know how did they keep such a stoic class and quiet strength about them in the face of what they were dealing with and not snap out. I'd like to know **Rosa Parks**, what made you keep your calm when they threw you off that bus. We as a people now have no idea what our forefathers went through to get us to this point. That's why I get so angry when I see some of our youngsters actin' a fool! Trust me, I wasn't there either, but I'm fortunate enough to have the kind of family members that were involved. My parents really weren't, but I had aunts and uncles who were. I have an uncle who's an ex Black Panther! So, I grew up knowing about **Assata Shakur**, **Angela Davis** and **Stokely Carmichael**. But, I think that one of the biggest things that I would like to ask is how did you keep the class and the dignity in the midst of people spitting in your face, and calling you names, and hitting you and sicking dogs on you? What kept you poised, where it didn't even phase you? I would love to know that kind of strength. I'm sure they're gonna tell me God, but I would just like to hear it from their mouths."

"I would be curious to see what **Frederick Douglass** would have to say about how things are now~in terms of our progress or lack thereof. I think his fighting spirit and his ability to analyze, I would love to have his analytical mind and give an assessment of where we are in this day and age."
~Kent Faulconer

Kent Faulconer
Actor

Kiki Haynes,

Actress

"Wow! I have never been asked that question before! I think I would want to meet with **Harriet Tubman**. I would love to have a conversation with her. She came to mind because I actually saw~from what I was told~ an original one of her hidden railroads where she would hide the slaves in Nyack, NY. My sister lives there. When I was standing next to this house, I was almost in tears~just imagining how many people came through there. How many people's lives she saved. And being a Black woman at that time, what gave her the strength and the gall to believe she could do something that was so profoundly against everything she was told she can do, because whatever that is~in today's society with the privileges we have as women, if she can pull that off, there should be nothing we women today can't do."

Michael Jai White & Tasha Smith,

Actors

"For me, it would be **Paul Robeson**. For a man like that to achieve what he did at the time period that he did it~I'd just be a sponge. I'd want to hear everything he had to say to me."
~Michael Jai White

"I would say **Dr. Martin Luther King** and **Malcolm X**. If I could have both of them at my dinner table a the same time, I would have so many questions about so many things. I can't even begin to tell you, but those are two people that I've respected and both of their passions to what they believed in. And to just talk about life, social issues, cultural issues, political issues, faith issues. I would have many questions and would love to hear their thoughts."
~Tasha Smith

Dining at OWN was awesome!

Courtesy of DepositPhotos/S. Bukley

I OFFER A SPECIAL SALUTE TO OPRAH WINFREY.
Because of her public endorsement of then-**Senator Barack H. Obama**,
the world finally saw an African-American elected President of The United States.
Thanks Lady O! You are a treasure. Keep makin' history.

77

"Big Sam" Williams Bolden,
New Orleans Musician

"The person I'd choose is **Prince**, and not just to talk about music, because he's a musical genius. I would want to make small talk about what do you do when you're at home on a normal a day. Do you go to the grocery store, movies and shopping malls? Do you dress in disguise so people don't recognize you? That's what would interest me the most."

~Big Sam (PS...this is my cousin)

"It would be **Frederick Douglass** because he suffered through slavery and experienced what it was to have freedom and ultimately have power as an ambassador involved in the government. And what it is to have that lynchpin between the haves and the have-nots within our own community, and the things you have to do to be successful and understand how to deal with challenges. He was a man with insurmountable challenges placed in front of him, but he ultimately prevailed."

Wendell Pierce
Actor

Wendell at the NAACP Image Awards nominees luncheon, January 17, 2015

Goapele,
Singer

"I have to say one of my dreams already came true. I got to have dinner with **Prince** and my family, and that kinda was like a childhood full circle exciting moment. I feel lucky that I've gotten to meet a lot of people that I looked up to~**Stevie Wonder, Hugh Masekela, Miriam Makeba**, while she was around. Dinner with Prince was great! He was so attentive to all the details being just perfect. It was beautiful." **~Goapele**

Naturi Naughton
Singer/Actress

"I would probably want to spend some time with **Coretta Scott King**. I would want to know so much about being the woman behind such an amazing time in history with **Martin Luther King**. She was also an opera singer. I would want to know how did she navigate doing so much as a woman, as a leader and carrying on the King legacy as well. So, I would want to talk to her."

Naturi Naughton at the 42 movie premiere in Hollywood.

Darrin Dewitt Henson,
Actor

In 1909, **Matthew Henson** became the first person to reach the North Pole.

"I can't just choose one person because there's so many pioneers, so many educators, so many black inventors and inventions. I think I would do a disservice by trying to chose just one. If I had a choice, it would be a collective sit-down beginning with **Malcolm X**, **Marcus Garvey**, **Martin Luther King, Jr**. So many people for me. I would say **Elijah Muhammad** as well. I would also go back to my ancestor, **Matthew Henson**."

Darrin, an ancestor of **Matthew Henson**.

Garcelle Beauvais,
Actress

"**President Barack Obama**. **Michelle**, because she'd probably kill me if I just invited him," she says jokingly. "And **Oprah** and **Deepak Chopra** would be my dinner guest." ~**Garcelle Beauvais**

Garcelle Beauvais is originally from Haiti.

White House Photo/Pete Souza

President Obama at a White House state dinner, chats with **Gursharan Kaur**, wife of **Manmohan Singh**, the 14th Prime Minister of India. **General Colin Powell** and others also present.

Al Jarreau
Legendary Jazz Singer

"Oh my goodness! Well, you know what? I'd like to sit down with **Martin Luther King** and **Tavis Smiley** together~if he could arrange that," he said with hilarity. "That would be a serious conversation about where we've been and where we're going. I think Tavis has a brilliant handle, him and Dr. West, on where we're going and what we ought to be doing. And certainly Martin Luther to talk about where we have been in our dreams and aspirations."
~**Al Jarreau**

80

Al & Eric J. at the NAACP Image Awards nominees luncheon, January 17, 2015

Shondrella Avery, Actress

Shondrella was elated when I told her about this book. She thought it was a great idea.

"Oh wow, that's an excellent question. I would first and foremost say **Maya Angelou**, just because I've been slated as being someone similar to her in my advocacy for education and I used to write poetry in high school. I would probably ask her, 'What would be the paradigm to continue to go on when you are up against so much adversity?' I know that there is God. I'm all-things Jesus Christ, but during this space when you are at six feet, you ideally look different. You are different. What keeps that process going? I would probably ask her that question in the midst of her dark moments. **Ruby Dee**. Just to have had that life and legacy. I had the privilege of meeting both of those ladies, but never had these conversation opportunities. But for Ruby Dee, just the whole thing between her and **Ozzie Davis**, keeping that marriage together for so many decades, especially in an industry where people are divorcing like its just going to the club. Right? We've lost sight of that."

White House Photo

Dr. Mayo Angelou & President Obama.

Nicci Gilbert, Singer

"It would definitely be **Dr. Maya Angelou**. And that conversation would just be how is it that I can be more fearless? How is it that I can be more phenomenal? How is it that I can impact my community in more positive ways? I admire her bravery. I admire her ability to just be a strong black woman who is nontraditional but fearless."

81

Rev. Dr. Michael C. Ellis, Sr.
President, Tennessee Southern Baptist Convention

"Obviously the run away choice would be **Dr. King**. But I would want to sit down with my great grandfather, **Morgan Taylor** and just listen to him share with me what it took for him to endure hard times and do it in a way in which it embraces people of all races. He was an entrepreneur when African-Americans didn't have the opportunities in Mississippi. And he took what he had and allowed God to use what he had to help him get to where God was taking him. He took his sons and leased them out to the white landowners like indentured servants, not for cash money, but for land. He ended up with almost 200 acres and didn't have to pay anything for it. His sons were the labor pay. And he left the legacy of land that the family still owns today including our Taylor/Jordan Family Park in Rose Hill, Mississippi. He was not just my great-grandfather, but yours too Eric J."

Dr. Michael & Lady Angela Ellis

May 10, 1900 - May 4, 1982

In July 2014, **Dr. Ellis**, my cousin, and the pastor of Impact Baptist Church in the Frayser community of Memphis, TN became the first black president of the Tennessee Southern Baptist Convention in its 140-year history.

Morgan Taylor, aka *"The Hawk,"* our great-grandfather. He and our great-grandmother **Willie** had 18 children.

July 16, 1890 - Dec. 8, 1979

Willie Lee Byrd Taylor, our great-grandmother. That's me, Eric J, in the white shirt. I loved being around my grandmother because I always had an interest in history, especially our own. Her mom, **Calla Byrd** and grandfather, **Willis Johnson** are on the front cover of this book.

Kita Williams, Mikki Taylor & Monique Jackson

"The two people I would love to sit down and have dinner with would be **Harriet Tubman.** There are so many great things she did for the slaves on the Underground Railroad. What was that like? That was a real dedicated mission. I would love to hear what Ms. Tubman's words of wisdom would be~especially back then. The other person I'd like to sit down with is **Madam CJ Walker.** If you don't know, she created the hot comb, the pressing combs. And I think that is the best thing in a black woman's life or any woman that has what we call kinky, curly hair. Not nappy. Kinky curly. She was the first black female millionaire and I would love to talk to her about that, especially during the time, number one~when black people were oppressed, and number two, when women didn't have a voice."

~Kita Williams

Editor **Mikki Taylor**, flanked by celebrity publicists **Kita Williams** & **Monique Jackson**

"Oh, my! That is such a tough question, but If I could spend a moment in time with someone from our past, it would be **Martin Luther King, Jr.** And to just sit at the table and drink up the wisdom to understand the vision and the passion that I might be~in the words of **Maya Angelou,** 'finer, better, stronger, more powerful.'"

~Mikki Taylor

"I'll say **Ella Fitzgerald**, because I would really want to know how they made it back in the day. How did they do it? How did they get through their times going through the (entertainment) industry."

Dorinda Clark Cole,
Gospel Singer

In 1826, **Edward A. Jones** graduated from Amherst College in Massachusetts and **John Russwurm,** an abolitionist from Jamaica, graduated from Bowdoin College in Maine. Not one black person graduated from their respective schools for the next 150 years! Jones became missionary to the colony of Sierra Leone in Africa and was its first naturalized citizen. Meanwhile, Russwurm, who's father was English and mother was a slave, became the first black member of a college fraternity. In 1827, he published **83** America's first black newspaper, *Freedom's Journal*, an abolitionist newspaper based in New York City.

Footnote In History

Mali Music,
Singer

MALI MUSIC & ERIC J. AT THE MERGE SUMMIT IN LA.

"**Martin Luther King, Jr.** I would ask him 'Why?' so I can get enlightened into his reasoning. Because his passion was unreal."

~**Mali Music**

"If I had an opportunity to sit down and have dinner with someone in history and ask a few questions, it would be **Imhotep** who lived from 2650-2600BC. (His name means the one who comes in peace, is with peace.) He was the chief advisor to the pharaoh **King Djoser** of the third dynasty and the architect who built the first step pyramid. He was also a physician, high priest and astronomer. We have mathematics, chemistry, biology, and many sciences that we know of. What other hidden sciences are there that have been hidden from us today that would increase the human potential. And how can we use the relationship of sound and vibration for manifestation. I'd engage him in conversations about those subjects."

Mariea Antoinette,
Smooth Jazz Harpist Extraordinaire

Affion Crockett,

Actor

Affion Crockett, in gray shirt, on the set as we discuss the movie *Haunted House*.

"I would like to speak to **Crispus Attucks**. I want to know what it was at that time, being a slave, that made you want to rebel the way that he did. What gave him the strength to say, unh, unh. I ain't having that no more, because I often feel like that in Hollywood. Hold on, these brothers are tapping to the same music that they want us to dance to and I'm not feeling that. So, I want to rebel a little bit. I wanna pop my collar and shake something up. So, I wanna talk to Crispus."

"I probably would meet with **Rev. James Cleveland**. My father taught myself and my siblings how to sing. And James Cleveland was an influence for that. So, to meet the person who influenced my father and gave us the love for gospel music, to be able to meet him and say 'Thank you for paving the way,' that would be kinda cool."

Maurette Brown Clark,

Gospel Singer

Israel Houghton,
Gospel Singer

ISRAEL AT THE LONG BEACH GOSPEL FESTIVAL, 2013

"Probably **Quincy Jones**. I think from a production standpoint and just his stories and what he's seen in music. I think I would enjoy that very much. What wouldn't I ask him? I would ask him his greatest moments and the moments he learned the most from."

On May 6, 1812, **Martin Robison Delaney** was born a free man in Charles Town, Virginia. Considered the first black nationalist, he was a renaissance man: An abolitionist, journalist, judge and doctor. He was one of the first African-Americans admitted to Harvard Medical School. And he was the US Army's first black major. His mother's dad was a Mandingo prince.

Publc Domain

Martin R. Delaney

Footnote In History

Maxine Waters,
US Congresswoman

"I think I would like to have dinner with **Harriet Tubman**, because I want to know where do you get the strength and the ability to keep moving, and to provide leadership in hostile environments, and with people attacking you and with you not knowing whether or not you can carry out the mission you have chosen for yourself? And how do you get the courage to lead a movement when you know that it is dangerous and anything can happen to you? I'd just like to hear where that comes from."

Congresswoman Maxine Waters and I at **Rev. Jesse Jackson's** gala in Beverly Hills.

Hanging out with Mr. Holden at VIP tent of the Taste of Soul Festival in LA.

Nate Holden,
Former CA Politician

"I would talk to **Paul Robeson** and reflect on the speech that he made at a peace conference in England when he said that the Black American would not fight a war against Russia or any other country in the conditions in which we live in America today. And they tried to prove him wrong of course, because then, the Korean War started and they integrated the Army at that point. After he made that speech, he came back and gave a speech in America in the Essix House in Newark, New Jersey and he said, 'I'll take not one step backwards.' He was saying I stand by my statement. I said it and I'm here to represent. Period. So, I like his strength. And I'd reflect on what's happening today in America and how with his influence, progress has been made by taking such a strong stand. He was such a strong black man. He influenced me in a way in which I was able to make a lot of changes in this country with my legislative program. That's why I stood firm. I never acted angry. I became effective. Ya see, anger won't do nothing for you.

Swin Cash,
Pro Basketball Player

Public Domain Photo

DR. DOROTHY HEIGHT
March 24, 1912 - April 20, 2010
Nat'l Council of Negro Women
Delta Sigma Theta Sorority, Inc.

Swin at an ESPN ESPY event in Hollywood.

"It would be with **Dr. Dorothy Height**. The first time I met her, I did not know who she was. And she knew who I was. She actually grew up the city right next door to mine. I would have asked her so many more questions had I known back then, but afterwards, I went and researched and learned a lot more about her. Just an unbelievable woman. Such strength, such power, such courage. She would be one person I would love to talk to. With the National Council of Negro Women, she was fierce. You look back at those old pictures of MLK, you'll see her to the right or to the left, and sometimes it's not about being seen, but it about just being there."

Ray Chew,
Music Director

Courtesy of The White House/Pete Souza

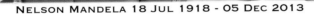
NELSON MANDELA 18 JUL 1918 - 05 DEC 2013

First Lady Michelle Obama & former South African President **Nelson Mandela** at his home in Houghton, South Africa.

"I'd like to spend an evening with **Nelson Mandela**. I'd like to talk to him about the struggle. He was the equivalency of a **Dr. Martin Luther King**, just in terms of sacrificing your body and your whole life for a cause. And that's a very special burden. That's a God-given type burden when you're charged with that kind of mission."

"**Malcolm X** and **Martin Luther King, Jr** would come right before **Barack Obama,** but it would definitely be those two because I think that they were morally grounded. They were inspirational, educational and they were warriors on our behalf. And to pick their brains coming from two different perspectives~talk about feeling fulfilled when you walked away from a particular meeting! If I sat down with Dr. King and Malcolm X, I don't think I would need much else to galvanize and energize me to be all I can be."

Stephen A. Smith,
Sports Journalist

89

Claudia Jordan,
Reality TV Personality

"I would have to say **Ms. Rosa Parks**. I would like to know how she fought to get out of the back of the bus to the front? But some of us embrace the back. And I'd like to know what made her stand up to the rules. I love people that kinda break the rules and go for it."

Claudia Jordan & I at the ESPN ESPY Awards red carpet in LA.

90   **Ernest Thomas**, aka "Raj," joins **Dr. Danielle Spencer**, aka "Dee," his "What's Happening" TV sister and I at her book signing at Stevie's in Tarzana, CA. She is a veterinarian based on the East Coast.

"Okay. Great question! I've always wanted to meet **Dr. Martin Luther King,** simply to ask him what kept him going when the road looked bleak; when thy bombed his home, when they harassed his family, when thousands were arrested, etc. I can see starting a movement, but pledging day-by-day to keep up the momentum and dedication takes a super King! By the way, your book is a brilliant idea!"

Dr. Danielle Spencer,
Actress/Author/Veterinarian

Dr. Benjamin F. Chavis,
National Newspaper Publisher's Association

"I have had dinner with him, but I would like to repeat the dinner with **Fidel Castro**. And the reason is because I believe that he played a key, pivotal role in the liberation of Southern Africa, including the nations of Angola, Namibia, Mozambique and South Africa. I witnessed first hand in the 1980s, how Cuban soldiers shed their blood and gave their lives for the freedom of Africa from the racism and oppression of apartheid."

Dr. Benjamin F. Chavis and I at the "Taste of Soul" sponsors reception in LA.

Danny Bakewell,
Civic Leader/Media Mogul

Frederick Douglass.
He was a publisher and a visionary.
I'd talk to him about that."

Danny Bakewell, publisher of the Los Angeles Sentinel 91
Newspaper and creator of The Taste of Soul Family Festival
and I at the "Taste's" sponsors reception in LA.

CCH Pounder,
Actress

"I would want to spend it with **Cuffy**, an African slave who lead the first major slave rebellion against the Dutch in Georgetown, British Guyana (February 23, 1763), which is where I was born. And I just want to know what he was thinking and how he got to that. (That day is Republic Day in Guyana which honors Cuffy.) In terms of international history, Cuffy; in terms of somebody local and down the road, I just missed **Coretta Scott King**, being able to talk to her. I'm always fascinated by the people that's right next to the power. Right next to dynamism; right next to inspiration, because they themselves have got to hold that person up as well, in a different way and out of the limelight. So, I'm always curious about that."

"I'm always fascinated by the people that's right next to the power." ~CCH

"That's a good question. **Rosa Parks**. I think that she was such a strong woman. I would just thank her, probably. I thought that was such a beautiful story of what she did."

Sydney Leroux,

92 US Olympic Gold Medal Soccer Player

Soccer star **Sydney Leroux** shows me her arm tattoos during an interview at "The Body" pre-ESPN ESPY event in Hollywood.

Colin Kaepernick,
Pro Football Player

QB COLIN KAEPERNICK AT THE ESPN PRE-ESPY "THE BODY" RED CARPET EVENT IN HOLLYWOOD.

"The one person I can think of is **Dr. Martin Luther King, Jr**. He was a great man and we owe a debt of gratitude to him for what he did for our people."

"**Jesus**, of course. And why, because He's Jesus! And then **Martin Luther King** because he was such a visionary at such a young age and what he did that we still benefit from. I was just love to sit with him and really get a chance to talk to him."

HOLLYWOOD POWER BROKERS
DEVON, FLANKED BY ERIC J & CHARLES KING, A FORMER PARTNER AT THE WILLIAM MORRIS AGENCY, NOW LEADER OF MACRO, A NEW MULTICULTURAL MEDIA FIRM.

DeVon Franklin,
Movie Executive/Author/Minister

Quinton Aaron,

Actor

"Wow! Very deep question. A couple of names come to mind: **Sidney Poitier**. Definitely **Martin Luther King**. And I'm a big **Maya Angelou** fan. I'd want to talk to them about their fields and about what they've been through. I love learning from people who've been through things that we still experience today. With Sidney, I'm just a fan of his as an actor. I watched a lot of his movies. So, it'd just be cool to meet him and learn from him as an actor and artist. With Martin: That's the man there! I definitely would like to meet him and get some words of encouragement or words of wisdom from the king himself. And Maya, on the poetry and artistic side of things, she was just so creative and so phenomenal! My mother was a poet before she passed and Maya Angelou was one of her heroes."

"It's actually the late great **Ruby Dee**. She was an amazing woman. She did so much for people, and for our culture also. I would love to just hang out with her to see how it was dating in the business, before social media of course. How she kept everything so rooted and grounded and still being in the upper echelon of all actors."

"I'd like to have dinner with the most famous black man of all times, **Jesus Christ**."

Reginald Hudlin,
TV/Film Executive

94

Eva Marcille,
Actress/TV Host

Josephine Baker in 1927.

Public Domain

Niecy Nash,
Actress

"**Harriet Tubman** was such a powerful woman. I'd like to know how she freed so many people! I'm curious to know what she was thinking. And **Josephine Baker** was fierce! I'd like to know about her journey in the entertainment business."

"I would say **Josephine Baker**. I really relate to her spirit because she was ostracized and she couldn't go into certain places. She couldn't perform in certain places. She was put down for the style that she had. She was very risqué. And people judged her for that. And she was amazing! She had to go to France to get work because America turned her away. There's many, but she's one of the ones I relate to."
~Dawn Robinson,
Former EnVogue singer

Dawn Robinson,
Singer

95

Ryan Clady
Pro Football Player

"Maybe **OJ Simpson** to pick his brain about what he's done in his career and in his life. He was a great player and he's had some things happen to him after football that's been kinda crazy but, I think it'll be fun to pick his brain though."

"The Juice"
OJ Simpson

"I relate to **King David** the most in the scriptures as far as him being a musician, a worshipper, but then a fighter and a warrior. And then having his struggles and keepin' it real. I would like to sit down and converse with him about how he did it. He still was very humbled. David was one who expressed all of his emotions but pointed it to God. He was like, '**Lord**, I'm hurting. Lord, I'm confused. Lord, I'm angry. He was one who's heart **God** said, *"He was a man after my own heart."* I would love to sit with David and pick his brain on just how he kept his focus God the whole time, but yet was a king. I'm the king of my house, a husband and father, but yet a worshipper."

Tye Tribbett,
Gospel Singer

DeLeon Richards-Sheffield,
Gospel Singer

"I would definitely pick **Martin Luther King**, just for the fact that I've had an opportunity to spend a lot of time with his family. And to see who they are really makes you want to know who he was. Other than how they portray him, but to know and really understand his thoughts and where he comes from."

~DeLeon

DeLeon Richards-Sheffield and **Dr. Bobby Jones** share a smile on the red carpet at the BET Celebration of Gospel in Downtown LA.

IT WAS AN HONOR WHEN **DR. RANCE ALLEN** TOLD ME HE WAS A BIG FAN OF MY JAZZSPEL TV SHOW WHEN IT AIRED ON THE WORD NETWORK.

"It would be **Dr. Martin Luther King** and all I would want to do is sit down and talk to him about whatever he wanted to talk about."

Dr. Rance Allen,
Legendary Gospel Singer/Preacher

97

Bishop T. Larry Kirkland,

AME Fifth Episcopal District - Los Angeles

Photo courtesy Library of Congress

Bishop Richard Allen and the Bishops of the A.M.E. Church:
The first independent black denomination in the US,
established in Philadelphia, PA in 1794.

98

In my estimation, it would be with **Bishop I. H. Bonner**, the presiding bishop of the Ninth Episcopal District where I was born in the state of Alabama. And my conversation with him would be, 'What made him so great, rising from the ashes?' Our parents were not educated. Children grew up without school or taken out of school to pick cotton, but yet he was inspired to become something. He was an outstanding bishop of the AME Church. He got the people out of jail in Selma when they had the Selma to Montgomery March. He was there and made friends with whites as well as leading blacks. I would have a conversation with him. I wish I had done that before he died.

In fact, he ordained me a preacher, long before I went off to college and studied for the ministry. But I never got a chance to ask him that question. As I reflect on it, I should have.

Richard Allen founded the African Methodist Episcopal Church. He walked out of St. George's Church because they were deprived of taking communion. They segregated it and said you (black folk) can't have it until whites had taken it. And therefore he walked out and bought a blacksmith shop and started the African Methodist Episcopal Church because they wanted to remain Methodist, but they wanted to keep their heritage as well. And that's why we in the AME Church, 3.5 million people to date, 9 thousand pastors, 6000 presiding elders, and 20 active bishops, and I happen to be one of the active bishops of the West Coast.

Definitely! Richard Allen would be at dinner with me, to find out what gave him the nerve to get up and walk out of that church~owned by whites! This was before slaves were freed. And he walked out of the church! And took a chance on his life being taken, yet he gave us a great denomination of which I am extremely proud of.

I would certainly like to include my father, the **Rev. H. E. Kirkland** from Birmingham, Alabama, and of course my mother, who was a missionary, **Mrs. Gladys Kirkland**. They are people I would love to have a conversation with. How they raised 15 children and all of us have been successful."

In 1816, Richard Allen became the
first bishop of the AME Church.

Ernie Hudson,
Actor

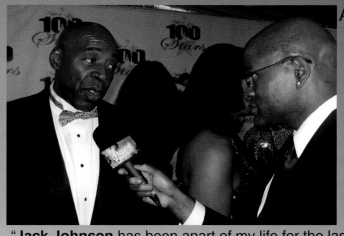

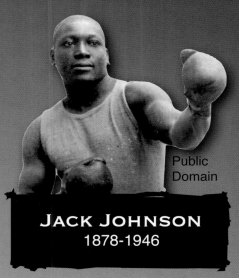

Public
Domain

JACK JOHNSON
1878-1946

"**Jack Johnson** has been apart of my life for the last 40 years. I've been fascinated that this man could live this life at that time, which is why I want to tell the story. I feel like he's talking to me and telling me that he needs his day. So, I would love to have an evening and a conversation with him. His is an amazing, American story. He was the first Black man to win the heavyweight boxing title in 1908. He paved the way for **Muhammad Ali**, **Sonny Liston** and others. He spoke five languages. He was a bull fighter. He was a race car driver when they didn't allow Blacks on the track. He was just an extraordinary man. He was a published author. He had patents on inventions. This is a guy who's just an extraordinary man and I don't think he ever got his due recognition. But I would love to have a conversation with him."

"I'd have to say **Martin Luther King**. I still listen to his sermons to this day. I got them loaded up on my iPhone. He was a guy that changed history. I don't know if it's possible, he changed the future. That's why we are standing here today. Sometimes I just sit back and meditate on him and his words. And it's unfortunate for him to be gone. And then seeing where we're at today. It's amazing because sometimes we plant seeds   and we don't get the harvest until years later. So, even though he's gone, we're still reaping that harvest. So, it's amazing just to follow him and try to soak up everything that he's put out there."

Brandon Marshall
Pro Football Player

Ernie Singleton,

Veteran Music Executive

BILLIE HOLIDAY

"It probably would be **Billie Holiday**. And why? Because at time when it wasn't cool to speak your mind, she did songs that were very revealing, that were very much about what was going on~*Strange Fruit* especially. And we're still strange fruit. Because it's that uniqueness of us, that I think bring so much validity to music. But it's also something about our music that I think has opened the door for **Obama** to be president."

"Oh my, there are so many people still living that I'd like to spend an evening with like **Michelle Obama**. But from the past~**Frederick Douglass**. Oh, there's so many things that I would ask him: His spiritual life and who inspired him."

Florence LaRue,

Legendary Singer

Vanessa Bell Armstrong
Gospel great

"I would have want to have dinner with **Mahalia Jackson**. She was such a pioneer and a trailblazer. I'd talk to her about her awesome journey."

Tachina Danielle, **Vanessa Bell Armstrong** and I after **Bishop Walter Hawkins**' funeral in Oakland, CA.

Vanessa Bell Callaway
Actress

"I would spend an evening with someone I never met: my great-grandmother. I knew my grandmother who passed about ten years ago, but I knew her well. I was very close to her. She was a fiesty lil' something! And I would have loved to have met her mother."

Shaun Robinson
Celebrity TV Host

"Since I just went to Paris, being at dinner with **Josephine Baker** would be fantastic. Just to find out about her struggles and what her life was like."

Footnote In History

Did you know that **Sistah Rosa Parks** wasn't the first black person to refuse giving up a seat on a public bus? Look up **Irene Morgan Kirkaldy**. In 1944, while riding a Greyhound bus, she was asked to give up her seat. She refused, and even resisted arrest! Her defiance led the Supreme Court to outlaw segregated seating on interstate bus lines. I hope these Footnotes In History inspires you to dig deeper. You just might find more treasures!

Anthony Anderson,

Actor

NAACP Image Awards nominees luncheon.

Eric J & Anthony

Anthony and TV One's **Alfred C. Liggins**

January 17, 2015

"**Frederick Douglass** and **Crispus Attucks**. Frederick Douglass, there's so many questions I'd like to ask him. How did he teach himself to read? What made him feel that that was something he needed to do? And Crispus Attucks. Why did you have to die first, sucka!" he joked. "Why did you jump out the window? Why did *YOU* jump out the window first!? And I'd add **Harriet Tubman**. And you can just imagine what our conversation would be." ~**Anthony Anderson**

Yara Shahidi,

Actress

102 **Anthony Anderson** and co-star **Yara Shahidi**, who has a 4.5 GPA and is a future Harvard student.

"That is easy: **James Baldwin**. I am a big fan of James Baldwin, I'm reading *Go Tell It On The Mountain* right now, and I've read *Sonny's Blues*. I've done a lot of research on him and I think what's amazing is he was living in this time of the civil rights movement and there was so much going on in Harlem, the Harlem Renaissance had just ended and to be a black gay man in America and the amount of scrutiny that he faced, but how he overcame it, it's just an incredible story. It would be amazing to hear it from him. I've read all the books. I have the James Baldwin last interview book, I pre-ordered it on Amazon. I think that's what the conversation would be about. To have such a large impact on the community is such an amazing thing." ~**Yara Shahidi**

Yara and her mother **Keri Shahidi**, an actress.

Dr. Joel & **Lady Yvette McLeod** of NDU.
(Learn more at NextDimensionUniversity.com)

Dr. Joel McLeod,
Chancellor/Next Dimension University

"The person I'd choose may be a surprise, but it would be **Marvin Gaye**. He was a great artist and he sang about situations that pertained to his people, including asking "What's Goin' On?"

Ann Marie Johnson
Actress

John Wall
Professional Basketball Player

"It would be **Martin Luther King**. I would want to know how did he stay so strong and so immensely prepared to go through all the tough times that he did. And I'd want to talk to him about how he came up with the speech, *I Have A Dream*."

"My mother and father who have since passed away. But my father, **Joseph P. Johnson,** was one of the first to integrate LAPD and my mother, **Ann Clay Johnson,** was a vice principal of an elementary school which was unheard of during that time being a woman of color. So, my parents really cleared the way for me to be able to do what I do. Out of all the people I can choose, I just want to sit down with them just one more time. I just wonder how they made it. How they persevered. How did they become the best parents a child could have and not even realize it? I didn't feel forced to do anything. My parents supported me unconditionally. I kinda want to talk to them about that and ask how did they learn how to do that."

103

Tanya Hart,
Celebrity Journalist

"This is really tough, but I would have to choose my family ancestor **Mary Ann Shadd**. She was Canadian and the first black woman to publish a newspaper in North America, *The Provincial Freeman*, in 1853. She was also the first woman publisher in Canada. She migrated there from Wilmington, Delaware and got very involved in the Canadian emancipation movement as an abolitionist. Our family once owned the post office in Buxton County in Ontario, Canada. I would love to talk to her. I've really been fascinated by her. She was my father's cousin. And the Shadd family is still in Canada. The irony is I ran into one of my cousins on the vineyard. Another favorite is **Frederick Douglass**. And because of our Boston connection, I would have loved to sit down with him. It seems like I have, because I have seen so many people portray his life. I feel like I should have known him. My dear friend **Lynn DuVal Luse** runs the African American museums in Boston and Nantucket, home of the first Black church in America. We've had these conversations many times. My husband, **Dr. Philip Hart,** was on the board of the African American Meeting House in Boston and he was one of the people responsible for renovating it along with the late **Henry Hampton**, who did *Eyes on the Prize*, and **Ruth Batson**, a noted civil rights and education activist. I have lots of stories, so this has great interest to me."

104

Matty Rich, Director

"Wow! That's a good one. Well, he's still living: **Sidney Poitier**. He's always been an inspiration to me. I watched his movies. He inspired me to direct. And he actually signed me into the director's guild. For someone who's not still here with us would have to be **Miles Davis**. He was prolific in his music as an artist. I had the opportunity to hang out with him during the *Jungle Fever* premiere. So, I got the chance to talk to him a little bit. So, he's always been an inspiration of mine. And then **James Baldwin**, a prolific writer. His storytelling, his writing and his novels definitely inspired me."

Willie Gault,
Former Pro Football Star

"Wow! If I had to just choose one, it would probably be **Dr. Martin Luther King** because he meant so much to the Civil Rights Movement and just the person he was. I think it would be very interesting to spend some time with him and try to get some of his knowledge and carry it on through the next generation."

In Memoriam

Dr. Andraé E. Crouch
July 1, 1942 - January 8, 2015

Stuart Scott
July 19, 1965 - January 4, 2015

"One person I'd love to dine with is **Muhammad Ali**, who I've met. People always talk about who are your heroes. Other than my dad, Muhammad Ali is at the top of the list~everything that he stood for. Like a lot of us, I grew up with him. Everything he stood for, I'm awed by it. The other probably is **Jackie Robinson**. Just what he went through. His fortitude. His calm. His strength. His integrity. His character. I would like to just sit and talk. It really didn't matter the subject. When it comes to people who have integrity and character, it doesn't matter what you talk about. It's just a matter of talking to them~hearing what they have to say. Asking questions and listening, and giving them what you have to say and see what their take and perception of it is."

Dr. Crouch was my personal friend and at his last birthday celebration on July 3, 2014, I told him he would be one of my guests at that dinner table along with **Frankie Beverly**, **Harriet Tubman** and others. While he was a gospel music legend, he was an even better person. On the last voicemail he left for me, he ended it, "*Your friend, Andraé*." Rest well with the ancestors, your friend, Eric J.

105

This iconic picture from Chicago after the 2008 victory will live for the ages.

A Salute To The History Makers
The Night I'll Never Forget

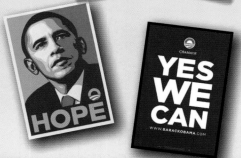

The most exciting night of my career came on Election Night, November 4, 2008, when then-**Senator Barack Obama** won the presidential election. My colleagues, **Tabitha Goodwin**, **Holly Fowlkes** and **I** had team coverage from three LA locations for my Jazzspel TV show on The Word Network. Of the 138 episodes I did, this was the most important one. The reality is: I never thought I'd see a black man elected President of the US!

We were at the New Orleans Vieux Carré Restaurant in LA's Leimert Park when CNN reported Mr. Obama was the projected winner. As **Stevie Wonder's** song, *Signed, Sealed & Delivered* played loudly, the place erupted like the Emancipation Proclamation was just announced! Tears came down as praises went up. At last!
What a night!

I anchored from the Obama headquarters at the Century Plaza Hotel in LA. Tabitha reported from the New Orleans Vieux Carré Restaurant and Holly reported from a house party with reaction. Because of my love for history, nothing will ever top this evening.

Honoring History

The Obamas stand by the edge of Lake Michigan viewing their hometown Chicago's skyline on June 15, 2012

Inauguration Ball dance in DC, January 21, 2013

Inauguration Parade ride in DC, Jan. 21, 2013

Photos courtesy of The White House Pete Souza

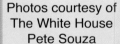

President Obama in The West Wing Oval Office

Bishop Charles E. Blake & President Obama at The White House

In Conclusion

I hope this book was a blessing to you and inspires you to bring out the hero in yourself. Or at least support the hero in somebody else. I honor all of the ancestors. This is my gift to their legacies. I hope it stirs up the gift in people all over the world. And stop waiting for the perfect time to share your gifts. There isn't one. You just have to make the vision plain and do it. That's what I did. Stop talkin' about it, and be about it. It's time.

As I look at all the pictures and people in this book, I'm even inspired, considering it was all done with absolutely no financial budget. But it was done with pure determination, knowing my purpose in life, and living up to it. If I can do this, surely you can do what you've been anointed and appointed to do. The cemeteries are littered with people who died with brilliant ideas. Don't be one of them. Now that this vision is out in the universe, I'm ready to go create the next project that will add light to somebody's life. I cannot rest on my laurels with the completion of this assignment. So, stay tuned for more.

When I started my journalism career as a 13-year-old sportswriter earning $3 per article with the Slidell (La.) Daily Sentry Newspaper in 1976, I had no idea I would still be doing this after all these years. And it's about to get better because I plan to create a TV series and movie inspired by this book. I'm just happy I persisted, even when family and friends suggested I go get a "real job," whatever the hell that is! Publishing this book is real. It didn't just create itself. So, rather than me looking for a job, I'm am building a legacy. And to do that takes a whole lot of skill and a tough hide. I love what I do.

Believe it or not, below is the first celebrity picture I ever shot. It was **Marvin Gaye** after his concert in San Diego in 1983. The tickets were only $12.50. He actually stopped and posed for me on one shot. I was in the US Navy aspiring to one day do what I'm doing. To date, it was the best I've ever attended. From Marvin Gaye to **Beyoncé**, my journey continues...

Marvin Gaye signing autographs after his 1983 SD concert.

I've served this nation. Now, I'm serving the ancestors.

Beyoncé invited me into their dressing room for an interview. I first met her and **Kelly Rowland** when they were 19 years old.

Please visit my website, DiningWithTheAncestors.com and share it with others. Also, purchase some of the other products as your support will help make the rest of the vision a reality. Respectfully, **Eric J.**

Don't Lose The Vision

This "Childhood Reporter" picture was taken Thanksgiving Day, November 28, 1974 in Pearl River, LA when I was 11 years old pretending to be a reporter. That's me on the far right, dressed up, holding my makeshift microphone, along with **Lorenzo**, my brother, **Jackie**, my youngest sister and **Hester**, my mom. My grandmother **Lucille's** trailer is the blue and white one. Ours was the brown and white one on the right. Although our trailer was repo'd, I thank God He didn't repo my visions and dreams~including this book.

Childhood Reporter: 28 NOV 74

My career has been decorated with 4 Emmys & 5 Golden Mike Awards from CBS. I dedicate them to the ancestors.

My mom **Hester**, my cousin **Magaline Penny** and my daughter **Aerica** supported me when I received a doctorate from Next Dimension University in Ontario, CA on August 17, 2013. What an honor!

Acknowledgements

First, let me thank some of the many people who have sown financially into my life, beginning with my former Navy buddy **Shahid Shabazz** and **Dr. Michael Stone, DBA**. These two fellas saw enough in me and the vision to invest. Without them, I'm stalled.

Nina Rawls, my friend, thanks for your kind support and encouragement. Thanks to my brother **Lorenzo Chambers** and my cousin, **Sherry Bolden**.

Additional thanks to:

Betty Watkins, Susan Perkins, Lucius McCall, Derrick & Mona Zinnerman, Sherri Bryant, Rev. Rodney Hunter, Dr. Steve Cooper, Dr. John Wells, Bishop George D. McKinney, Jr., Dr. Cecil "Chip" Murray, Brian Peters, Jackie Thomas, James Byndon, Lisa Lake-Grossman, Angelina Washington, Dackeyia Q. Sterling, Mike McCoy, Airickca Gordon Taylor, Dr. Lezlee Hinesmon-Matthews, Rita Fannings, John L. Mason, Karen Hill, Dr. Larry Moore, Lee Bailey, Fern James Crossley, Dr. Leonidas Johnson, Dr. Maceo Crenshaw Dailey, Rev. Kenneth Curry, Douglas Bender, Mimi Banford, Perseus Poku, Dr. Ephraim Williams, Gina Paige, Yvette Kaufman-Bell, The Fowlers~Terrie, Dorothy & Yolanda, Floyd A. Smith, Jackie Chambers, Joyce Wiley, Patricia Craig, Dr. Rose Parker Sterling, Dr. Rani DuBois, Harold Corsey, Arthur Gulley, Jr., Dawnn Lewis, T'Keyah Crystal Keymah, Willard Pugh, Shawna Chambers, Tanner Gray, Nate Payton, Lisa Loftin, DeVonna Law, TJ Dunnivant, and to all who helped in some way.

Thanks to the following publicists:

Erma Byrd, Edna Sims, Terrie Williams, Lynn Jeter, Phyllis Caddel-M, Nicole VanderPloeg & Dominic Morea.

This book is dedicated to my beloved mother, Hester Ducre and to my talented and loving daughter, Aerica Noelle Chambers. I love you eternally.

Trace your DNA. Find your roots at:
AfricanAncestry.com

The Illustrators

1) **Chelle Brantley**, illustrator of the W.E. B. DuBois/Ja'Net Du Bois art is a portrait artist, painter and illustrator. A native of East Bay Area Oakland, she's a gifted artist who resides in Northern California. Visit her website at http://ChelleBrantleyArt.com

2) **Clarence Pointer**, illustrator of the Frederick Douglass dinner, is a professional realistic pencil artist. Among his commissioned works was a portrait of Rosa Parks for Edwards AFB. Visit his works at ClarencePointer.com.

3) **Andre Harris**, illustrator of the Marcus Garvey/Cedric The Entertainer and Cleopatra/Dawnn Lewis drawings. A graduate of The Art Institute of Atlanta and The American Intercontinental University, Andre has established himself as a force to be wreckened with in the art world. Learn more at AndreHarrisDesign.com.

4) **Stevon Sample**, illustrator of the Mahalia Jackson/Kelly Price picture is a artist and owner of Dominion Multimedia in Exmore, VA. Established in 2010, the company also does graphic illustrations and billboards to name a few. Search for him on Facebook or e-mail DominonGraphicArt@Gmail.com.

5) **Mike Fields**, illustrator of the Sheryl Underwood/Marlon Wayans picture, is a self-taught oil painter from Columbus, Ohio. Mike has been painting professionally since 2007 and has been gaining recognition around the globe. His subject matter is "People of Substance" meaning historically or currently. Visit him at FieldsOfArt.net

6) **Quatrick Williams**, illustrator of the Sojourner Truth, Yolanda Adams, Tamar Braxont and Sheryl Lee Ralph drawing is a conscious visual artist born in Shreveport and currently residing in Columbus, Ohio. Visit him at QEWProduction.com.

7) **Keenan Chapman**, illustrator of the Kentrick Lamar/MLK/Malcolm X picture is one of the nation's most gifted artists. The LA-based artist says art is his therapy and vacation. Learn more at ArtBattles.com.

Please visit and support our illustrators.

*Shout out to QuickStudy.com for inspiring Footnotes In History.

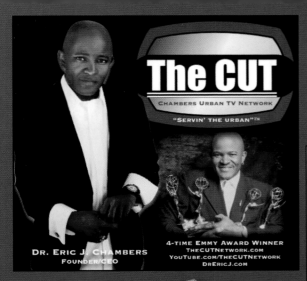
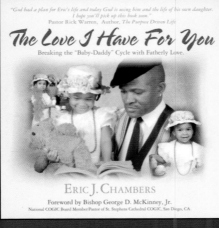

TABLE of CONTENTS